TRUE LIES

DISCLAIMER

This is a work of fiction. Names, characters, places and incidents either are products of the author's imagination or are used fictitiously. Any resemblance to actual events or locales or persons, living or dead, is entirely coincidental.

Rosewood, Ron 1941
True Lies / Ron Rosewood

ISBN-13-978-1492374930
ISBN-10-1492374938
Edited by Doris Benjamin
Published by Highway 1 Publishing
Printed and bound with www.createspace.com

RON ROSEWOOD

TRUE LIES

AN ANTOLOGY OF BIZARRE LOVE AFFAIRS

HIGHWAY 1 PUBLISHING

TABLE OF CONTENTS

BEYOND THE CALL
OF DUTY

CHAPTER 1

Mavis entered the prison interview room, put her attaché case on the table, and then came around it embracing Ken who welcomed her warmly. Holding her close, he squeezed her tightly against himself and whispered, "How have you been baby?"

"We shouldn't be doing this." Mavis sighed as Ken slid his warm gentle hands beneath her blouse. She felt her breasts move down and forward as he unsnapped her bra. She felt him lift it, along with her sweater, up and over her breasts, resting on her neck and shoulders.

"Stop me." Ken released her for a moment, and then he savagely pulled her up against him. Hurriedly slipping her faded blue jeans down her lower torso, he encountered no resistance as he feathered kisses on Mavis's neck and ear lobes. His hands moved thematically as if playing a smooth musical instrument.

The unrestrained pleasure he was generating sent Mavis straight to cloud nine. Her nipples hardened on her heaving breasts; her breathing quickened. If there was any desire to stop him, it give way to sheer pleasure. She wanted him; she needed him; she was going to have him. "The hell with the consequences," she thought. Consequences were of no concern to her now.

They moved together as one, racing each other to the place they both yearned to be. There was no need to communicate verbally; their bodies imparted it all. They reached for the feeling and knew it was time to luxuriate in the ultimate feeling that only two people in love can experience. They gave each other everything they had, it was daring, it was naughty, and it was wrong; but it was fantastic!

"We shouldn't have done that!" she scolded Ken as they readjusted their clothing. She kissed him once more as she went back to her side of the interview table. "Now, let's get down to business."

Mavis was a 33-year-old psychologist at New Haven Prison, had been counseling Ken for several months. Mavis remembered the first time she met him. His striking good looks highlighted by his black hair and deep blue eyes sent her into a flutter even in those first few moments upon touching his hand.

Ken was a 'two time loser' as the guards described him to her. He had served two years for assault. Now he was 5 years into a ten-year manslaughter conviction for taking the life of the same man he had assaulted earlier. Apparently, Ken could not understand why his wife, Beth, preferred brown eyes to blue eyes.

Beth divorced him 2 years after he began serving his current sentence. He was eligible for parole in another eighteen months. Being a model prisoner, he was confident that he would be successful in his application when the time came.

"I can't wait until I can apply for parole." He remarked, as he lit up a Rothman's cigarette.

"I wish you'd quit smoking those fucking cigarettes!" she grumbled. "This is 2006, you should know better!" She pushed his ashtray over to the furthest side of the table.

"I'll give it a try when I get out. In here I have only two pleasures, smoking and you know the other!" He winked at her.

"Seriously Ken, we have to stop this fooling around, it could affect your parole, and my job."

"These guards know what's going on. They choose to overlook these things. They're men they understand. The only thing they wish to see is the backside of me as I finish my stretch and walk out those prison gates." Now, what have you got for me in those files there?"

"I have to complete an assessment document on you, so it is ready to submit with your parole application." She drew a 10-page packet of sheet papers from her case.

"Give it to me, I'm a high school graduate for God's sake, I'll fill it out." He reached out and yanked the form out of Mavis's hands. "Give me a pen will you."

"Why are you so volatile? We have to show you are reformed

and rehabilitated. "She handed him her pen." Acting like a crazed animal, won't impress anyone."

"I'll be fine." Ken began answering the questions, marking off the best possible answer to each question. In twenty minutes he was done. "Honey, you have to sign it on page ten."

Meekly Mavis, took the form and the pen and after glancing over it, she looked up. 'I don't think this answer on how you handle anger management is answered correctly. I would have scored it as 'making progress; but still needing to improve!' "

Ken stood up, eyes glaring, "Look you know it all, bitch, take the damn thing and turn it in." He reached down and upended the interview table, adding, "If you don't get me out of this fucking cornflakes box on schedule, you will be one sorry cowgirl."

"It sounds like you're threatening me!" Mavis glanced at the door she could see the form of a guard standing there. He was ignoring everything that happened. He was not about to tangle with Ken!

"I'm promising you, not threatening you, Sweetie. You know how anxious I am to be released, so we can be together; Isn't that what you want? Make sure you get me the hell out of here. I don't know if I can wait much longer."

She nodded, as she helped Ken stand up the table. "I'll get you out; just keep a lid on your temper. Now what do you mean you can't wait to get out? Don't do anything stupid. In eighteen months you will be a free man."

Ken advanced toward her "Look, you bitch, do everything you can and more, to see it happens. Do you read me?"

She backed up towards the door and knocked on it with one hand while watching Ken moving closer. "Stay back, Ken, I don't want a scene."

He stopped and stood still. Seeing fear in her eyes, he began turning on the charm, calmly whispering, "You have it all wrong, Sweetie, I just wanted a goodbye kiss. By the way how are things coming on the day parole request we filed?"

It's in the works. I expect it to be approved by next week. I'll see you then at the same time. "Mavis replied, as she hurriedly tapped on the door once more.

Ken relaxed "Okay Sweetie, I'll be here waiting."

⊱

Chuck, the guard, opened the door. Mavis made her way out to the main office. The guard escorted Ken out the other door to the holding cells. "It's time for your basketball practice. Do you need to go to your cell first, or shall we proceed directly to the gym."

"The gym will be fine, sir." Ken obligingly moved up along the guard. "How has the trout fishing been?"

"The lakes are just beginning to produce a few nice Bass."

"I miss my fishing."

"Perhaps when your day pass comes through we can do a morning outing to a local lake. A few innocent fishing trips may look good on your sheet."

"Let's do that, Chuck," I need to get all my ducks in a row here. I'm somewhat worried about Mavis she's getting jittery."

"It certainly didn't look and sound like that earlier," Chuck winked at Ken. "I' wouldn't mind a crack at that filly."

"Wait, until I'm done with her and I'm out of here, Chuck." Ken snapped, "You know the way it works, give the ladies what they like and they keep coming back for more." He chuckled. "I'll actually miss this place; it's really not that bad! You just have to look for opportunities that can be exploited, like that bitch Mavis."

"It all depends on your real intentions. If you're snowing her, I'd say you are handling yourself very well. She's really hooked on you. Mavis would do anything for you."

That's what I'm counting on, big fella!"

CHAPTER 2

Mavis was finishing Ken's paper work, as well as, having her third cup of coffee. She questioned her motives as she typed up her recommendation pages. Was she compromising her professionalism because of her on going affair with Ken? Of course, according to the ethics of her association, she was up to it to her armpits in shit. The prison rules clearly forbade such relationships. How could she carry on? Should she ask to be transferred to another facility? Would it be wise for her to ask someone else in her department to take over Ken's case file?

She was mulling over all these questions, yet in her heart, she knew she could not break up her relationship with Ken. Why, she thought, did he have such a strong hold on her? Mavis had taken courses relating to the topic of women becoming fixated over their male partner. The reasoning offered was that women tend to see the potential good in a man and they usually minimize his faults. In other words the old axiom of *he isn't a bad guy, he just does bad things*, is the excuse they use to justify continuing a risky relationship.

Did Ken have real potential? Mavis thought so; he had been a firefighter for twelve years with the New Haven south-side station. He had several commendations for bravery over and above what duty called for. He had been interviewed by the press and T.V. stations about his exploits. If that wasn't potential, then what was? Did he have to walk on water to redeem himself? Sure, he lost his temper and killed a man. That could not be set aside. Would he do it again? Only Ken, his conscience and future circumstances could answer that.

Why was she so attracted to him? Was this obsession with him unnatural? Was it his sexual prowess that fueled her obsession? Certainly, that was part of it! Women need what women need and Ken had the wherewithal to satisfy her most intimate wishes. That should not be the sole governing factor. Did he remind her of her dad? In looks, he did; the black hair and blue eyes were common to them. The quick to anger trait was a flaw that was also shared by them. Maybe that was the key!

Mavis remembered the many times when she was a youngster and she heard her dad, Jack, demanding his way with her mother, Beth. If it wasn't about sex, which it was in many instances, then it was about money. If not about money, then it was about the radio being too loud, or the neighbor's pit bull barking up a storm. Beth, of course, fearing physical harm would do all she could to placate Jack. Was that lifestyle ingrained in her mind to the extent that she subconsciously felt it was the normal way to live? Was that the reason? Was she looking for a 'father figure'? That could be the explanation for her irrational behavior.

She stopped daydreaming and settled down to prepare her letter of recommendation for Ken.

June 21, 2006, New Haven Prison Authority, Board of Corrections
Subject: Kenneth Harris
In connection with Mr. Harris' application for a weekly day pass, I have made a determination of his progress over the past several months. I can now say that in my professional opinion Mr. Harris could have a day pass of say ten hours on the provision that he accompanied by a prison security staff member.
Mavis Martin

Mavis felt uneasy about being pressured into making her recommendation, especially after that morning's table upsetting episode. *Why should I take all the heat?* She thought, *let the board read between the lines and deny it.* They were not ignorant on the guile ways of incarcerated prisoners and their methods. However she yearend for the day that her and Ken could be finally together and lead a normal happy family life. Even start a family! She printed the document and together with an envelope took it up the hall to the warden's office.

Mr. Jim Trent, the warden, was alone in his lavish mini-board -room office. He looked up as she entered. 'Ah, Miss Martin, I was just about to ask you over. We have to discuss the applications that Ken Harris has filed.

In addition I have my recommendation for day passes here." She handed him the letter.

Trent, read it once and then again. Looking up he asked Are you sure Harris is trustworthy enough to be granted this pass? I've seen his kind before, all gentleman on the surface and a virtual maniac on the inside." He looked away as he continued." There's, shall we say a rumor, that you and Ken are in a less than professional rela- tionship. I'm not judging you, people are people; however, don't let your feeling for this guy cloud your judgment."

"Rumors are the order of the day around here sir! I wouldn't put too much stock in them. As you well know serious relationships between staff and inmates are forbidden. As for the letter, I think I have made a reasonably prudent conclusion Sir; as you know the board can rule against it." She bluffed him by saying "I would have no objection to you advising the board about your concerns relating to my letter. That would make it more their decision, not mine."

"I see what you mean Mavis; however that would be undermin- ing your professional status. We don't want to do that. Leave it with me I will decide on what I will do, when I hear the board's questions at next week's meeting. In the mean time let me know if there is anything my office can do to minimize your involvement with Mr. Harris. We have other staff members including Max Stephens, who can take his case off your hands."

Mavis minimized the thought. "Ken, I mean Mr. Harris, has only a few months to go until parole, so I think I should keep him on my case-load. He'll be gone and hopefully reintegrate into society."

Trent replied, "Okay, Mavis, however, if the board denies the day passes then I will be reassigning Mr. Harris to Max. I don't want to place you in danger!"

Mavis nodded slightly and left without any further comment. Next week would be a telling session with Ken; she hoped she would be up to it. More precisely, she hoped Ken would be up to it!

Ken was looking forward to the prospect of getting a weekly day pass. An outing like that would break the monotony of the prison routine. It would be refreshing to have a relaxing fishing outing. He imagined sitting in a canoe with a paddle in his hands and a fishing rod set for trolling on the ready waiting for a bass to strike. He had been an ardent sportsman in his younger days, hunting and fishing had occupied all his free time.

Unfortunately, Beth was unenthusiastic about his need to 'Kill God's Creatures' so she kept reminding him of his primitive urges. Mind you, she didn't object to his "other" primitive urge. He wondered where she was, and what was she doing? He hadn't seen or heard from her for over two years now. Perhaps it was best to forget about her, she was the reason he was in prison now, if she had stayed out of her relationship with that brown eyed bastard, they would still be together. *Maybe I offed the wrong person*, he thought as the rage he felt because of her infidelity resurfaced in him.

He hoped Mavis' influence and recommendations would be enough to get him the day passes. That would be his chance to put an end to the day-to-day misery of prison life. In 37 years, he had made one mistake; was that a reason for denying him a second chance? After all, there were many far worse criminals than him in New Haven. He felt it was unfair to lump him in with them. He was only defending his family's honor when he 'took out' brown eyes. If he hadn't done it, some other jealous husband would have eventually done the same.

CHAPTER 3

One week later

Mavis approached the interview room with a combination of hope mixed with trepidation. Standing guard outside the door as usual, was Chuck.

He greeted her with a wide knowing smile, saying "Time for our exercises, is it?" as he winked at Mavis.

Mavis blushed but felt she had to respond. "Do I look or and comment on your every move Chuck? No, I don't! So why don't you just go a few steps away from the door and scratch yourself anywhere you want."

"I'll wait until you're free, you scratch better than me."

"Be careful what you wish for; now move aside before you get hurt."

"We shouldn't be doing this." He teased, repeating her last week's moaning. Then he stepped aside opening the door for her," have fun now" he said as he was closing it after her.

Hi Babe!" Ken was in his usual cheerful mood anticipating his sexual treat.

"Not today, Ken. Not with that creep out there listening to every sound. God I wish someone would stick one to him."

Ken whispered, "He'll get what's coming to him, just leave it to me." Ken smiled at the thought of 'offing' Chuck.

Mavis nodded without commenting, she hurriedly continued with her reason for coming, so Ken wouldn't keep on about Chuck. "I have good news for you. Your day pass has been approved. In fact, in two days you have a four hour escorted pass."

"I thought I would get a ten hour pass, why four instead of ten?" Ken was angry.

"Look, Ken, you can have a nice outing in four hours, the city is only fifteen minutes away. Don't forget the budget has to cover the one on one salary cost of an escort."

"You're worried about the God damn cost to the prison budget? Whose side are you on?"

"Yours of course!" She diverted his attention. "Who do you think will be accompanying you?"

"Chuck I presume, next to you, he knows me best?"

"Perhaps, you should talk to Chuck if you want him, he may be able to volunteer to baby sit you."

"Don't be funny with that baby sitting crap. Will I be able to have some private time with you?"

"Sorry Ken, not this week, I'll be working here. Maybe next week you'll get a ten-hour pass that will enable us to get together at my place after I finish here. That would be super!" She relished the thought of having Ken perform his magic over a two-hour period.

Ken turned hostile, "You bitch, Mavis, you set this all up so it wouldn't work out for us, didn't you?"

"To be brutally honest with you, Ken, I went beyond professional guidelines to even get you this pass. Now calm down before you create a ruckus and they revoke it. That's all I have for you today. I'm out of here. I'll see you next week." Mavis picked up her case and left. She heard Ken spouting off as she passed Chuck in the hallway.

"Women! They're all the same. They use you to get what they want and then they spit on you as if you're garbage! "

Chuck grinned at Ken's comments and teased Mavis "Trouble in paradise, I see."

"Do your job, and go get him out of there, before he trashes the room." Mavis replied as she scurried, fearing Ken might attempt to charge after her. She heard Chuck restoring order in the interview room.

"You're right, Ken, women are all selfish bitches, now forget her and let's go get an honest cup of coffee from the cafeteria. We can talk about your day pass and make some plans. I'm certain they'll let me be your escort. I know how to pack a good time into a few hours."

Ken was fuming, "She'll pay for this, believe me! I don't take shit from anyone. Look at all I've done for her during the past months. Who the hell does she think she is?"

"Just cool it, Ken, creating a scene here will not help your record. Now let's plan that fishing trip you've been pining for."

⊷

Mavis was shaking as she entered her office. Trent was walking by. Glancing at his watch he realized she was back half an hour earlier that usual. "Hi Mavis, how did that go?" He helped her to her office chair.

"That guy is scaring me! I hope you instruct your escort to be super alert."

"I'll put Chuck on it; they seem to understand each other. Don't worry what can happen in four hours?"

"I won't want to take a guess. Maybe it's my imagination, but! I will feel better once they are back from Ken's outing.

⊷

Ansonia Reservoir was teeming with bass according to the local anglers. Chuck loaded his canoe on his SUV along with fishing gear for two and a few sandwiches and beer. He wanted Ken to be well entertained. In his mind, Ken got a rather harsh sentence for a justifiable killing. He proceeded to the prison and signed Ken out at 7 A.M. "Ready for some bass fishing?"

"You bet!" Ken responded exuberantly as he climbed aboard. They were at the lake unloading the gear and launching the canoe within a half hour.

"Here Ken, put on a life jacket." Chuck said as he threw one over Ken's way. He elected not to wear one, as he was going to be doing the paddling. He was an excellent swimmer. He had been well trained in water rescue by the two emergency departments he had volunteered with.

'Which part of the lake are we trying first?" Ken asked.

"The North-west corner has some medium to shallow areas, I always do well there." Chuck turned the canoe away from the dock and began the fifteen-minute paddle to that area. "Troll as we go, you may just tie into one, the deep water is their place when the waters begin to warm up."

Ken, fastened a green flat-fish lure to his line added some weight about six feet above it and cast out the line allowing about eighty yards of line out to enable the lure to reach the lake's deeper levels.

In about ten minutes as they were crossing the middle of the reservoir, Ken had a huge strike. He set the hook and began reeling in what seemed to be a good- sized fish. Not being used to canoeing, he leaned over and lost his balance. The craft overturned, Ken realized his folly as he too was flung into the water. He wasn't worried the canoe had floatation and all they had to do was hang on to the overturned canoe and dog paddle themselves to shore. Chuck swam a short distance retrieved a paddle and swam back to the watercraft. "Ken where are you?" he hollered out when he didn't see his prisoner.

"Right behind you, Chucky boy." Ken replied in a low calculated tone as he swung the other paddle down on Chuck's head, striking him with baseball bat like velocity. Chuck collapsed, his body went limp and he slumped forward face down floating on the lake, with only a quarter of his body above the surface. Ken grabbed the other paddle letting his paddle drift away. Chuck's body began sinking beneath the lake's surface. Ken hurled a few last words at Chuck's corpse as he retrieved the SVU keys and wallet from Chuck's pocket. "So you'd like a crack at that filly, would you? Well, my friend, you might have dreamt about that, now, tell me how did it feel, was she as satisfying as you expected, maybe better. I hope you enjoyed the experience, you bastard! You'll never know how good she is." He single handedly grabbed the gunnel, jammed the paddle under the seat and dragging the craft with one hand he dog paddled toward the shore.

Luckily, for Ken no other boats were in the vicinity so within twenty- five minutes he made his way ashore. After wringing out his clothing, he then put them back on, and righted the canoe. Then he, waited an hour until his clothes were half-dry, he waited then paddled the righted canoe back toward the dock.

He beached the canoe about a quarter mile before the dock and dragging it up into some tall grass and brush. Making his way along a lakeshore trail, he walked up to the parking lot and to the SUV. He found some clothes that Ken stored behind his seat. He put them on, got in the vehicle and calmly drove out of there. He was set; he had a vehicle, gas in the tank, credit cards and cash in his pocket and at least two hours of get away time. Finding some quarters in the ashtray, he stopped at a phone booth and called the prison, asking for Mavis.

"Mavis speaking, how may I help you?"

"You already did that baby, now be sure you are at home tonight, better yet meet me at the Days Inn motel at four o'clock. I'll be watching for you. You will get your wish for being together. By the way pick up some red wine on the way" Ken hung up.

Mavis was speechless. She looked at her watch. Ken still had over two hours on his pass. *What did he mean by his call? Had he been stupid enough to make a break for it, how did he overpower Chuck? Should she report her thoughts to Trent, the warden? What were the repercussions for her, if indeed Ken escaped? Would she be found culpable? Should she meet him? He sounded like he had an exciting late afternoon plan. Was her own safety at risk?*

Mavis gingerly made her way down the hall to Trent's office. "Sir, I have to leave a half hour early today. My work is all done."

"Sure, you've been good at staying late now and then. Go ahead call it a day. I'll stay until Harris and Chuck get back. I want to talk to Chuck."

CHAPTER 4

Mavis drove home gathering a few personal items, freshening up and changed into something sexy. She had just enough time to drive the ten-minute drive to the motel. Pulling into the motel's parking lot, she saw Ken standing near the office entrance. His clothes looked familiar. *Oh my God, that's Chuck's Hawaiian shirt,* she recognized it from a Luau the prison held for staff last fall, *what did Ken do to get here?* Shivers of excitement ran up and down her spine. She walked over to where he was waiting, the usual smoldering cigarette between his fingers.

He smiled, "Over here babe, we have room 212 upstairs at the end."

"What have you done Ken?"

"I'm on a day pass, remember, let's say I got an unexpected extension!"

"What about Chuck. Is he with you?" She knew the answer to that question.

"He's in LA and, he wouldn't be bothering us anymore."

"Did you kill him?" Mavis demanded to know.

"No, not at all, we had a boating accident, I survived, and he did not. It's that simple. Now let's go to our room, time's a wasting."

Don't you think we should report the accident?

"What for, it's over, nothing can save that jerk Chuck." Ken led her up the stairs to unit 212. He took the wine from her as they entered the room. "Make yourself comfortable while I serve out the wine."

"I'm not so sure I'm in the mood. You know that news about Chuck."

"Well honey, just get in the mood! He snapped, and then continued, "Hey, these things happen. Here, relax." Ken handed her a glass of wine. "To us Honey, and to a lovely evening." They clicked glasses.

"Turn on some music Ken; we have to set the mood here." Mavis took another large gulp of wine. This was not what she expected. There were too many unanswered questions to Ken's being able to be with her when it was almost past his deadline. She forced her mind back on their reason for being here. There was no harm in a couple intimate hours with her man.

Trent was getting nervous. Chuck and Ken were half an hour overdue. He called the Chief of Security. "Any sign of Harris and Chuck?"

"Not yet, I'll try his mobile phone." In a couple of minutes he called Trent back. "No answer Sir."

"I'm worried, the guy's a living time bomb. Chuck had a rifle in his SUV, if Ken gets it and is cornered there is no telling who else may get hurt. Do you have any idea where they went?"

"I overheard them talking about going fishing, but not where."

"That's fair enough, you know some of the guys that talk fishing with him. You follow up with them. I'll stay here in case Chuck calls. If he 's in trouble, try and arrange a meeting with him."

The Chief hurried down the hall to the cafeteria hoping to find Gillis there who was Chuck's best fishing partner.

Mavis, lay on the motel bed shifting her eyes from the ceiling and, looking over to the semi sheer curtains over the window. Imagining that Security was lurking nearby. She felt like the fool she was. *The Goddamn man was lying the entire time I knew him.*

Ken, sensing she was not fully into their lovemaking session, began using rougher and rougher thrusts with his body to get her attention." Come on baby, get with it."

Mavis pretended to get excited and soon was faking an organism that sent Ken over the hill and down the other side. She breathe a sigh of relieve as they separated their bodies and lay back. Ken reached for a smoke. Mavis was beginning to realize her decision to meet Ken, was the biggest mistake of her 33 years.

CHAPTER 5

The Chief and Gillis, came to Trent's office. "Gillis where did you go fishing the last time Chuck was with you?" Trent barked.

"Ansonia Reservoir, why?"

"He may be in trouble, he was escorting Ken Harris on a day pass. We think they went fishing. Take two other guys and head up there and see if there are any sign of them. Perhaps somebody saw them or their vehicle in the area. Report back to me ASAP."

"Right, Sir!" responded Gillis as he turned and went back to the cafeteria, poured his coffee down a nearby sink and summoned two others to follow him to the vehicle compound. "Come on guys, we have a missing inmate."

Arriving at the dock the men spread out and began questioning the few people in the area. Being a weekday only one other boat was out on the lake. Gillis hailed them with a mega phone. "Return to shore, we have an urgent message for you," he fibbed. The boat turned and raced toward them. Gillis directed his men to go a half mile down the trail one on the left the other on the right. Look for anything that may be hidden in the brush, Chuck had a red canoe. Watch for debris floating in the water, here take these binoculars with you," he handed each of them a pair.

He went over to a municipal employee who was painting a railing on the dock. "We have a missing inmate, did you see any one or anything, they were in a grey Ford SUV?"

"The man's face frowned and then lit up. "Maybe, I did! When I arrived there was a vehicle like that parked here. I went across the road for a coffee and chatted with the clerk for perhaps fifteen minutes." When I got back the SUV was gone."

"That's it then, thanks. When my men get back tell them I've gone to phone in a report."

The man nodded, and resumed his work.

Half an hour later one of the security officers returned. "I found a red canoe hidden in the bushes, the only other things were one paddle and one wet life jacket, no other equipment of any sort."

"That confirms it, something happened and only one person made it back, guess who it may have been?"

It's confirmed, one person is on the loose with Chuck's truck." Trent agreed. "That bloody lying Harris, no good in him at all, why do we bother trying to help these burnouts?"

"Let's get going, I put out an APB on the vehicle, now let's wait for results. There are three roads out of here in three directions, and he has a two hour start on us."

"Not good!"

"You said it, and there was a rifle in the SUV."

Trent was pleased with the results of the investigation so far. He hoped another lead would come in soon, pinpointing Ken's location. It was two o'clock, something should materialize before dark, unless Ken holed up somewhere. He went to see Mavis; then realized she had gone home early.

He went to the night clerk, receptionist "Tell me where does Mavis live?

She gave him the address, and phone number. He dialed, no answer. Trent left a message. "Mavis, come back to the office right away, I think Ken has gone AWOL. He turned back to the receptionist "The guys may return yet, have some faith in the system, you know Chuck, they could be in a pub somewhere!

"Good faith! That's a trait, these men lost years ago." The receptionist added.

Trent nodded, "And Mavis, can consider herself under suspension, until we convene a hearing and look at all the issues leading up to today's breach."

"I think she would expect that Sir. I'm sure she will cooperate fully in any way she can."

۞

Two hours later a call came in from the state police, they had apprehended Ken at a checkpoint on the New York Sate state border. He had surrendered without a struggle. There was no sign of Chuck, his wallet, credit cards nor any weapons. The only statement Ken had volunteered was that there was a boating accident and only he survived. He saw an opportunity to flee and in a moment of weakness he drove off in the guard's SUV.

"Moment of weakness! Now I've heard it all." Warden Trent was relieved that there had been no further bloodshed or injuries to any of the enforcement personnel. "I had a talk with the police and they are searching the reservoir, it could be days before they ever find a body, especially if life jackets were not used. Until then we can't ascertain if this is indeed an accident or a homicide."

"Phone Mavis again and see if she can report to me."

Mavis had just returned home. "Is there news?" Mavis feigned appearing worried.

"Yes, the Warden will update you. I'll connect you."

"Mavis, Listen. The initial crisis is over we apprehended Ken"

"Is he okay, he isn't hurt is he?"

"You mean Chuck, don't you?"

"Well yes, both of them," Mavis realized she was still harboring feelings for Ken. Trent listened to her with amazement on his face. "I think under the circumstances you should stay home, even though it's safe now. You can consider yourself under suspension. I will advise you of the hearing, it may take a week or more depending on the search for Chuck. Is that clear?"

Mavis realizing the seriousness of her situation, asked, "Do I need a lawyer?"

"I would say that may be prudent, you want to minimize your exposure to charges."

"What kind of charges?"

'Breach of Trust, might be one. Aiding or assisting in a break out could be considered. Like I said protect yourself, don't talk to news reporters or anyone," he paused "not even your cat" he added, to make light of the matter, "you can't trust cats."

Mavis, made a face at the mirror image in front of her, "you can't trust anyone, can you?"

CHAPTER 7

By midnight Ken Harris had been returned to New Haven, he was uncooperative, realizing his best course of action was to play dumb. He performed the part masterfully.

"So I took a ride in a prison guard's personal vehicle, sue me , take everything I have." He smirked. "I'm not saying another word without a lawyer. Now get me some food I haven't eaten all day!"

Warden Trent nodded to Gillis, "get him a couple of sandwiches and a coffee from the cafeteria."

"Hey Gillis, I take that with a creamer and two sugars." Taunted Ken.

Gillis looked ready to tear him apart. Trent motioned with his hand to Gillis that clearly indicated *'go on, don't get into it.'* Gillis raised his eyebrows and left for the cafeteria.

Trent was alone with Ken, who still had manacles on his hands and feet. "Tell me one thing Ken. What role did Mavis play in to-day's and the past few weeks' events."

Ken smirked. "I banged her eleven times, tomorrow would have been a dozen."

Let's stay on topic. Now what did she that would implicate her in all of this?"

"She played the role of a dummy! What broad in her right mind would take someone like me seriously. These do-gooders think they have the magic touch. They pull down their panties a time of two, make a few moaning sounds and they think we are putty in their hands."

"Again what precisely did she do that helped you?"

"She got me a day pass. She recommended it."

"Did you tell her why you needed a day pass?"

"Sure I told her I was going to make a break for Canada. Is that what you wanted to hear?"

"If it's the truth, then yes, if it isn't then no, so which is it?"

"Ask the bitch, only she knows if she over-recommended me. Look at me now! I'm in here facing at the least some addition jail time and no possibility of parole, what did I get? Trouble, that's what. All because of that stupid bitch, why didn't she do her job and recommend against a day pass? We would both be at home sleeping without a care in the world."

Trent saw there was nothing this self-proclaimed angel could add to the case. Gillis came back in the room. "Lock lover boy here back in his cell, let him dine on his sandwiches in there, and put that coffee in a paper cup. We don't want him slashing his wrists, and oh yes leave him chained up for the night."

Ken objected, "That's cruel and unusual punishment, you can't do that!"

Trent replied. "Cruel and unusual! So now you're an expert on cruel and unusual! If I had you back in Texas where I come from, you would have something to complain about. No, rather you wouldn't be complaining at all, we would have taken care of business the first time you killed someone. Take him away." Trent spat in his wastebasket, to emphasize his sheer disgust with Ken and his *'I have rights'* attitude.

What did Mavis see in this scumbag? He asked himself as he closed his office door and called it a day.

By noon the following day, the evidence gathered showed a clearer picture. The second paddle had been retrieved. One edge of the blade was streaked with blood and some hair had lodged in the fresh crack in the paddle , enough to try a match with Chuck's DNA. The fishing gear was recovered in part, the second life jacket was found undone, and most important the area of where to search for a body had been confined to an area of several acres, rather than several thousand acres. Dragging operation had already covered the shallows and police divers were combing the adjacent deeper waters.

The call from the mobile police trailer came in at 1.30, "we have located Chuck's body."

Trent was precise "Take it to Yale Hospital, they have a forensic training unit there. I'll notify the coroner."

"Roger that."

CHAPTER 8

Three weeks later

The Coroner's report was in, the victim's death had been caused by trauma to the head. Matching the paddle to the head wound indicated with 90% certainty that it had caused the trauma. Since it was unlikely a self -inflicted wound, the only conclusion the coroner could make was that it was caused by a person, or persons unknown. That placed Ken in the hot seat, literally, he was facing the death penalty if convicted. The police were waiting for the DNA evidence to make a solid link from the paddle blood and hair fibers to the trauma on Chuck's head. Charges would follow.

Mavis was contacted by the police detective assigned to the case. He arrived at her apartment at 10 A.M. "I'm detective Jim Burnside" he flashed his badge.

Mavis stepped back and turned to introduce her lawyer. "This is Arnie Silverman"

Burnside was blunt. "We've met." He didn't appreciate Silverman's tactics. Silverman , instead of working within the laws and applying them fairly, always relished finding a "weasel hole" escape clause that in several instances freed an obviously guilty person.

Silverman chuckled. "Another of my many admirers." To Silverman, it was just another day at the office, *win some lose some*, was his motto . Prosecutors eventually learned, to their dismay, that this little jovial legal beagle used his subterfuge to put his opposition to sleep while he picked their theories to pieces with legal challenges. "Let's get started before my client forgets everything she knows." he suggested.

"May I record this interrogation?"

"May I receive a copy of it by this afternoon, Silverman countered." Burnside, nodded.

Silverman, spoke into the microphone , " Burnside nodded approval for my client getting a copy of this tape by this afternoon."

"Stop the theatrics, Arnie, do you see a jury anywhere?"

"Just practicing!" Arnie retorted.

"Now, Miss Martin, how long have you been acquainted with Ken Harris, presently housed at new Haven Prison.

"About seven months."

"How often did you meet with him during that time."

"Not much at first, then more often in later months."

"How many times a week, say in the last three months?"

Mavis blushed, "Most of the time once a week, occasionally twice a week, it's all a matter of written record in the prison journals."

"I know I've been inspecting them! And why did the visits escalate in the last three months compared to the first four?"

"Mr. Harris was filing applications for parole hearings and for day passes. I was asked by the Warden to do assessments of Ken's, pardon me, Mr. Harris' mental state and progress, to show he was worthy or not, of being recommended for approval of his applications."

"And that takes three months?"

Silverman quipped in "If she says it takes three months, then it takes three months, she's the expert, I don't see any degrees in psychology stamped on your forehead."

Burnside nodded, "Fair enough." He looked at his note pad. "Did Mr. Harris influence you to put in a favorable report for him, say more positive than you would for any another inmate?"

"I thought I was objective and fair, I certainly felt he deserved an evenhanded ruling."

Now Miss Martin, are the rumors circulating about you and Ken Harris having a love affair correct ?"

"What's love got to do with it?" Silverman interjected, smiling at his reference to Tina, Turner's hit song by that name.

"Let Miss Martin answer the question."

Mavis looked at Silverman who shook his head negatively.

"I decline to answer that question."

"You just did," Burnside concluded, flashing a slight smile.

"Objection."

"We aren't in court yet , Arnie."

"We are through here, Mavis, stand up." Silverman turned to Burnside. " I'll pick up my tape at 3.30 p.m."

Mavis looked at Arnie, after Burnside left. 'What happens now?"

You will be called as a witness against Ken. They will probably want you to say in some way that you over recommended Harris' progress, don't agree to or say that, it's a subjective thing that could be argued both ways, let the jury draw its; own conclusions. I'll try and mitigate your involvement."

"Will I be charged?"

"They will no doubt threaten to charge you to get you to agree to testify. I'll negotiate that part on your behalf."

"What about my Association?"

"There will be a hearing, you may lose your license to practice in this state. You needn't worry there are many other states where you can apply and be accepted. One mistake won't bar you for life everywhere"

"So, you think I was negligent?"

"I can't dismiss the possibility. How else could I defend you , if I didn't look at both sides of an issue."

"Is that the way it works? You reach an opinion about how guilty I might be?"

"We mitigate damages to your person or your reputation by striking the best deal we can broker for you."

"You mean, I won't get off Scott free."

"Christmas gifts are free. However, it's not Christmas yet!" Arnie was back to joking. "Not from what I know so far. Tell me, did you sleep with this Harris guy, or not?"

Mavis nodded affirmative.

"That is the main question, you will be asked, at all three enquiries. You will have to answer all. By not doing so, you do more damage, than by admitting to the truth. We can argue extenuating circumstances."

"What do you mean?"

"Ken had power over you to the extent that it clouded your judgment."

"That's true! I can see that now."

"There is your pat answer. Or the one I will propose to you if it doesn't come up in your questioning."

"How confident are you Arnie?"

"I'm 99.9 % certain the Sun will rise tomorrow morning." Arnie patted her on the shoulder. "Don't worry until I say worry. I'll contact your association and ask that they hold off on any disciplinary hearing until the police investigation is finalized. I will also tell them you will not be doing any professional work until they give you a clearance. Agreed?"

"Yes, that sounds like the right action to follow."

CHAPTER 9

Three months later

Robert Woods, the prosecuting attorney, for the New Haven County , began reviewing the file on Robert Harris, charged with first-degree murder. Also attached to the Harris file was the file of Mavis Martin, recommending charges of Breach of Trust, Aiding a fugitive, and conspiring to commit murder.

After reviewing the files he instructed his staff to proceed on a charge of first-degree murder against both Ken Harris and Mavis Martin as co-conspirator. In his mind there was sufficient evidence that Mavis Martin knew Ken Harris's plans to engineer an escape, and any offenses committed by him while doing so, made her culpable. Seeing Arnie Silverman was defending Martin, Woods knew he had to prepare his case with utmost care to ensure the wily defense attorney didn't reach into his bag of technical arguments and foil the prosecution.

The charges were prepared and filed, the first court appearance was to be held, 10 a.m. Wednesday, September 13, 2006. Judge Alfred Darling would be presiding. The name " Darling" did not match his reputation as a hard-nosed courtroom veteran. He had been a successful prosecutor for twenty -five years before being elected to his present position four years ago. He was seeking reelection in a year.

This outcome of this case could make a big difference in him getting support from the voters.

The Courtroom had more than its usual number of spectators and reporters. The case had gotten National interest. Judge Darling wasted no time, after the charges were laid he addressed the defense table, "how do the defendants plead?"

Arnie Silverman replied for Mavis Martin. "Not guilty, Your Honor." He was about to continue speaking.

The judge cut him off at the knees. "Sit down."

Turning his attention to Jill Conrad, the defense attorney for Ken Harris, the Judge barked. 'Let's hear it Miss. Conrad."

"My client pleads not guilty, your Honor."

"Nobody's guilty! What a relief!" The Judge retorted. "The defendants are remanded in custody, pending their trial."

Arnie Silverman, spoke " Your Honor, on the matter of bail for my client. Is it too harsh to not grant bail, it's her first ever alleged offense."

"You mean alleged murder offense Counselor" he paused "I'll tell you what, you can mitigate the harshness by visiting Miss Martin in lockup, be sure to take her a cookie." He banged his gavel. "Bailiff send in the next case, please."

Mavis was frantic. "Mr. Silverman, Can't we appeal the ruling on bail?"

"Yes, today was a mere formality with the laying of the charges. I'll argued before a magistrate that your not a flight risk, you own your own home, and have cooperated fully with the investigators. Beside that I am applying to severe the cases, since you will be expected to testify at Mr. Harris' trial."

Silverman was successful in obtaining bail of $ 500,000 for Mavis, and separating the trials. Ken Harris was to be tried commencing on January 2, 2007 and Mavis Martin on March 5, 2007. Mavis would testify at Harris' trial in as far as she could without incriminating herself.

Ken Harris was turning on the charm with his defense lawyer, Jill Conrad. He had chosen her from the public defenders' list, not for her prowess, but for the fact she was a woman and he might get more sympathy from a jury if he had a young enthusiastic, female, lawyer in his corner. After his first few sessions with her, Ken realized that she would not be easily manipulated- that was the downside. He did form the opinion that she was a dedicated lawyer and would research every case and decision that compared to his case. She went to work and suggested to Ken to have the charges reduced to non-premeditated second-degree murder, which would take the death penalty off the table, and add perhaps twenty years to his sentence.

"I'll be 69 years of age by the time I'd be released, fuck that nonsense. This was an accident, challenge the evidence and put some doubts in the juries' minds."

"I understand Mavis will be testifying against you. That could weaken your defense greatly."

"Tell her attorney that anything she does to weaken my case will be paid back in spades when her trial comes up. That will take care of 'Little Miss Bitch,' she's no threat, one look from me and she'll shrivel up like a dried prune."

"Don't underestimate a woman's fury, after all you more than likely cost her a career."

"She enjoyed the ride while it lasted!" Ken chuckled. "You should have seen the bitch enjoying herself, whenever we were getting it on!"

"Let's not get too graphic here, Mr. Harris."

"Why, am I turning you on? Do you think of me while in bed?"

"Hardly, now let's stick to the facts here. Do you want to testify? I am leaning towards leaving you off the stand."

"Screw that! I can be my own best witness. I'll have the jury, crying at the injustice they see as my trial continues."

"Don't underestimate the jury; a couple of hard working types will nail you to the wall when they see your cocky attitude. We'll have to prep you for questions, so you can explain clearly that you did not murder the victim."

"Like I've maintained all along, it was a terrible accident." Ken Laughed.

"Keep that tone, and there might be a terrible hanging a few years from now!"

Ken sobered up, he saw her point, this was his life he was gambling for. It was time to take his lawyer seriously. "I will work with you Miss Conrad. So what do we do next."

"We'll prep you during the next week, take a Christmas break, and then we go to trial and select a jury beginning on January 2nd."

"Whatever you say, Missy," Ken could see there would be no goodnight kisses emanating from Miss. Conrad. What a shame, he thought as he watched her slim, trim body walking down the hallway and out of the building.

CHAPTER 10

Feb. 2, the trial begins

The court had ordered thirty individuals to attend the jury selection process. As usual, Jill Conrad could see that several already held, in their hands, exemption certificates from doctors or similar documents from employers or others.

The jury selection progressed, excusing four people for medical or planned vacation reasons. That left twenty-six, twelve women and fourteen men. Jill reasoned that she would select middle-aged women. They would be more sympathetic towards the defense's arguments for conviction then older men. Only as a last resort would she consider choosing any younger male person, as they would burn Ken Harris to a crisp given the opportunity.

The first potential juror was a retired man with a degree in accounting. Jill asked him if he had seen press reports and if he could render a fair verdict based solely on evidence to be presented. The man answered to the effect he had was aware of the general details; however, he had not drawn any conclusions. After a few more questions, which indicated the man was used to dealing in facts, Jill listed him as acceptable. . The prosecution also accepted him.

The answers given by the accountant had set the pattern and jury selection proceeded quite quickly. The defense rejected a narrow-minded pastor for obvious reasons. The army retiree of thirty years service was promptly excused by the defense. The undertaker thought to be too smug, was also dismissed.

The nurse was, accepted by both the prosecutor and the defense.

Jill rejected the philosophy student as too immature. The car sales-man was considered as too easy to persuade. Neither party wanted him. The theatre manager possibly biased by crime movies was rejected. The entertainer/singer obviously on some high-powered prescription tranquilizers was excused as well.

The twelve people chosen as acceptable consisted of seven women and five men, the two alternates were men. All the jurors were between thirty-five and sixty-five years of age. Jill was pleased with the jury as selected. She felt they were all mature logical people who would consider the legal points very carefully and not be drawn into the prosecution's suggestions about this being a well planned and executed crime.

The next morning as Jill entered courtroom seven, the defendant Harris was already at the table. The prosecutor and his team were ready. Jill took a slight step back and smiled when she saw Harris. Harris was sitting there with a neatly trimmed black beard streaked with silver, his black hair stylishly trimmed. Dressed in a light gray suit, powder blue shirt and dark blue tie, he looked like a movie version of college professor, a picture of innocence. The only features missing were horned rimmed glasses, and a flower in his lapel. Jill approached him and nodded approval at his stylish appearance. He stood up as she took her seat. Then he quietly sat beside her.

Robert Woods surveyed the drama as it unfolded "The son-of-gun will have a positive influence on the jury with that appearance. I wonder whose idea triggered this well groomed above suspicion outer shell " Robert began muttering to his assistant. "There is nothing that can be done at this time; we will have to handle the matter through questioning and innuendo as the trial proceeds. Perhaps the jury will see through his facade."

Over in the jury box all the jurors' eyes were gazing at the defendant's appearance. The spectator gallery was buzzing with excited comments. They expected to see a cold heartless murderer; instead they saw a man that they would readily walk up to and engage in conversation had this been a cocktail party rather than a courtroom.

Unfazed, Judge Darling, came marching in, declaring the court in session. Judge Darling began his instructions to the jury, finishing with, "You are hereby instructed that at this time the defendant is presumed innocent, and that the presumption of innocence does not change until the jury concludes deliberations. Jurors are not supposed to abandon the presumption of innocence until they have heard all of the evidence pertaining to the case."

He turned to Woods "Is the Crown ready to commence?"

"Yes, your Honor."

"Is the defense ready?"

"Yes, your Honor." Jill replied.

"Your turn, Mr. Woods," The Judge leaned back, ready to listen to opening statements.

"Your Honor, Ladies and gentlemen of the jury. The prosecution will clearly show through the evidence collected and the testimony of witnesses and others that on Friday, June 23, 2006 at approximately 9 a.m. the defendant, Ken Harris, did willfully murdered the victim Charles Dumont.

Mr. Harris, out on a day pass from New Haven Prison, and Mr. Dumont , with his guard, were canoeing and fishing on the Ansonia Reservoir. Within less than an hour Mr. Harris engineered a supposed canoeing accident and Mr. Dumont lost his life. The prosecution will clearly show that Mr. Harris seized his opportunity to take advantage of the mishap, and that he murdered Mr. Dumont.

Subsequently, Mr. Harris fled the scene and stole the victim's vehicle, and was at large for approximately 24 hours. Does that sound like the act of an innocent man? Quite the opposite! It shows the wanton disregard that the defendant had for human life. The choices he made on that day clearly indicate that he had one thing in mind on June 23, 2006. He was intent on making good his escape, in whatever manner, and at any cost in human life that would be necessary to enable him to accomplish that goal.

Ladies and gentlemen, of the jury, I implore you not to be lulled into distraction by the defense's claim that Mr. Harris is a poor misunderstood man, he is anything but that. He is a heartless, calculating, murderer that has only one goal, to project an image of innocence, so as to plant a seed of doubt in your minds." Don't fall for their explanations, interpretations and twisting of the facts in the case, as they try to build a defense for an indefensible crime. Thank you Ladies and Gentleman. "

Judge Darling, nodded to Jill Conrad to begin her opening statement. She began,"Ladies and Gentleman of the Jury, the prosecutor has painted a precise picture of the crime that my client Mr. Harris is on trial for. Was the Prosecutor there, no! He wasn't. He has based the majority of his statement on conjecture and unproven description of what he, his staff, and the investigators, supposed happened! As we go through the evidence and testimony of witnesses, it will be clear to you that the facts themselves will show that my client was powerless to save Mr. Dumont, his first duty was to ensure his own safety.

We will show that the death of Mr. Dumont was a freak accident. The charges against my client are greatly overstated and unsubstantiated, that should in your minds create a reasonable doubt as to his guilt. We look forward to dealing with every piece of evidence and the testimony of the prosecutor's witnesses and experts. In turn the defendant insists that, he not only wishes to testify on his own behalf, but that he demands that he be allowed to do so. I ask you is that the action of a man with something to hide? I say not, it is the action of a man that believes he has been falsely accused of a crime that he did not commit. Thank you Ladies and Gentlemen of the jury." Jill took her seat, she liked the reaction the jury portrayed by their body language as they had leaned forward in their seats listening intently to her opening statement. "We got them thinking" she confided to Ken as the Judge adjourned for a lunch break.

Judge Darling halted proceedings. "We will reconvene at 2 o'clock. Court is adjourned."

CHAPTER 11

The first witnesses were routine. They showed that Ken Harris was picked up at the prison and left in the presence of the victim. The defense conceded that was so. The lake conditions were established to be calm, the weather was clear and sunny. There were no contributing natural circumstances that contributing to the event.

The Coroner, Colin English, was the next to testify. The prosecutor went through the report with him, "Your report states death had been caused by trauma to the head."

"Yes."

"What caused the trauma?"

"A blow from a paddle to the head ."

"How certain are you?"

"I'd say 90% certainty that it had caused the trauma."

"Could the blow been self inflicted?"

"Almost impossible, in my opinion."

"Why?"

"The paddle would have had to been held short, near the blade. With that short a swing there could not have been the velocity needed to split a head open, as was the case here."

"So it was impossible?"

"Yes"

"No further questions."

Jill Conrad approached the box. "Was there any direct evidence in your report that indicated Ken Harris struck the blow?"

"No."

"Could you ascertain the time of death?"

"No, we know that it happened between, 8 a.m. on the day of the fishing trip and 12 noon on the next day when the body was found."

"That's 28 hours of time?"

"Yes, that would appear to be the case"

"So you can't say within an hour or two of when death occurred?"

"I'd be speculating?"

"Speculate!"

Colin English hesitated then ventured a guess, "Between 8 a.m. and 2pm that same day when the empty canoe was found, assuming the victim was not one of the persons that came ashore with the craft."

"So, in all likelihood death occurred during those eight hours?"

"That would be my determined guess."

Jill Conrad, realized she had not done her client a favor by narrowing down the time factor. She attempted to cover up the fact by quickly fielding another question. "Could the victim have been dumped in the water, still alive and then left there still alive and conscious, while the other person left the scene?"

"If he was a strong swimmer, he could have easily swam the five hundred yards to shore, so I would say that is not what happened?"

"Is it possible, that after the defendant left the scene, some one else came along, with say a Seadoo craft and perhaps have committed this crime?" The jury leaned forward intent on the answer.

"Possible, yes, probable, no!"

"No more questions," Jill had introduced a probable cause element into her defense.

Jim Burnside, the investigating detective was called next. Woods, the Prosecutor, was counting on his testimony to tie Ken Harris into the case. " Detective Burnside, tell the jury what your investigation uncovered?"

Burnside flipped up his first page on his clipboard stack of notes. "The DNA on the paddle matched the victim's so the paddle was the murder weapon. The victim's credit card was used by the defendant at the Day's Inn Motel. The motel clerk identified the defendant's photo. As the person that used the card. The Clerk also identified Miss. Mavis Martin as meeting the defendant near the office entrance and then going with him up to the second tier of motel units. The defendant's DNA from the bed sheet stains, was recovered and matched to him. The defendant had clothes on that were identified by the victim's wife as being her husband's clothing. The defendant was in possession of the victim's vehicle when he was arrested. The defendant was fleeing northward when arrested." He looked up, "That is pretty much it, Sir."

"I'd say that is pretty much enough!" Exclaimed the prosecutor as he turned to face the jury.

"Objection! The Prosecutor is introducing an opinion!"

"And a darned good one it is, Miss Conrad!" The judge was not leaning her way, "objection overruled. Your witness Miss Conrad."

"No questions, of this witness." Jill Conrad wanted Burnside off the stand and gone, before any more damage was done to her case. "Your Honor, the Defense requests a ten minute recess."

"Granted, court is adjourned for twenty minutes, take your time, Miss Conrad."

Miss Conrad took Ken to a private office, " Look Mr. Harris, this is not working in your favor. I suggest you give me authorization to discuss a deal for you with the Prosecutor."

"I suggest you start doing your work, bitch!' Ken replied.

"I'm representing you in an unwinnable case, Sir! Start listening or you will be facing a death sentence!"

"Do you think that Woods bastard will give me a break, he is after my hide and so is that Goddamn Judge, they are railroading me straight into a gas chamber."

"Then we agree! Let me attempt to get a reduced charge, or at least an agreement to take the death penalty off the table."

"Let's see how the rest of the day goes. Then I will let you know!"

"If they pile up any more evidence against you, the jury will hand you themselves."

"Funny Lady, like I said I'll let you know at the end of the day." Ken was not budging.

CHAPTER 12

Robert Woods called, Warden, Jim Trent, to the stand. He began by asking the witness's opinion on Ken Harris's demeanor. "Did the defendant ,in your opinion, conduct himself in a controlled manner?"

Trent hesitated before answering, "Most of the time he was well behaved."

"Would you explain to the jury the instances when he was not well behaved?"

"He had volatile outbursts if someone did not agree with him. He would upset office or cafeteria furniture and threaten to assault those that stood in his way."

"How frequently did this occur?"

Trent looked at his notes, "Eight times in the three months prior to June 23."

"How did he treat the women staff?"

"He was somewhat more respectful toward our women staff."

"Why, would you say that was?"

"He considers himself a ladies' man, you know good looks, quick smile, and a sharp wit."

"Was one of those women Mavis Martin, the psychologist in charge of his case?"

"Yes, they seemed to get on well."

"Would you say they got on 'extremely' well?

"Yes, that word would describe their relationship!"

"Can you clarify that statement?"

"Not specifically, but I can say that when I asked her if she wanted off his case, she objected. She wanted to remain involved in his applications and therapy."

"Is it a fact that there were rumors about Miss Martin and Mr. Harris having an affair."

"Yes, there was a rumor; that is why I suggested a change in Mr. Harris' psychologist."

"So you for one believed it?"

"Believing rumors was secondary; it is my job to minimize those sorts of occurrences, whether real or perceived.

"Here are the assessments Miss Martin, generated on Ken Harris. Would you verify that these are copies of the originals."

"Yes, those are my initials on the upper right hand corner of both documents."

"Did you have reason to examine these in connection with your regular duties as Warden?"

"Yes, I review all forms of that nature."

"Now, looking at this letter of Miss Martin's supporting the defendant's day pass application. Did you discuss it with Miss Martin, and if you did what was the nature of your exchange of words?"

"I indicated that Mr. Harris , did not deserve the assessment he was receiving from her?"

"What was her response?"

"She informed me that if I suggested to the deciding board to 'read between the lines', and if they turned down his application, then she would be personally clear of the decision."

"What did you gauge from that response?"

"That Mr. Harris was manipulating or threatening her in some manner. I told her in no uncertain words that if his day pass was not approved, I would be, for her own safety, removing her from the case."

"Did she agree?"

"She nodded affirmatively."

"No more questions of this witness."

Jill Conrad, rose and walked directly to the witness box. "I have only one question Warden Trent. If you deemed Mr. Harris a risk as you informed Miss Martin, then why did you initial her reports as satisfactory?"

'Miss Martin is a professional psychologist; I would have been undermining her opinion by over ruling her decision. I told her of my opinion she, in part, chose to ignore it."

"So, it's her fault, Mr. Trent, that Mr. Harris received a day pass?"

"I wouldn't go that far, however, yes, her report was an important factor in granting of the day pass."

"You're the Warden, are you responsible in any way?"

"As the Warden, yes, I must say there is a responsibility issue for me. That will be under review after this case is concluded."

"No further questions."

'The witness may step down." The Judge looked at the clock. "Court is adjourned until 10 o'clock tomorrow morning."

Mavis was informed that afternoon that she would be the first witness the following morning. She had an uneasy feeling about her role. She, of course, had to protect herself from incriminating herself; nevertheless she still harbored emotional feeling for Ken Harris, and did not want to cause problems for Ken and his lawyer. She had spoken with Arnie Silverman who had, straightforward, advice for her. Tell the truth as best you can; however, if a question comes up then claim the right not to answer it on the basis that it might incriminate you. The jury will figure it out, and be aware of what you did or said by your silence."

But, that makes their case against Ken even stronger!"

"That is Miss Conrad's problem, she can ask the jury not to speculate. Bear in mind your testimony should add to the case against Mr. Harris, but it should not make the case against you stronger. I can't do more than be there, if you are stuck for an answer and I just remain still, then claim the Fifth Amendment. If I agree that you should answer the question truthfully then I will lean forward in my seat. Is that clear?"

"Yes, if you don't lean forward, then I clam up."

The Prosecutor, announced , '"The court calls Miss Mavis Martin, to the stand."

Mavis, dressed in a medium blue business suit stepped forward and was sworn in."

"Miss Martin, your professional qualifications are well known to the jury, so we will dispense with repeating them here."

Mavis nodded.

"Now Miss Martin, we'll deal with the day pass application. "Did the defendant pressure you into over stating his character and behavior?"

Mavis glanced at Ken Harris at the defendant's table. Harris was sitting there relaxed, and almost beaming, as if happy to see her. There was nothing threatening in his manner. " No not unduly."

"Explain that answer?"

"Of course all applicants want to be successful in obtaining a day pass, so they verbalize their feeling and encourage the staff to be generous in their assessments."

"Were you 'generous' in your assessment of Mr. Harris?"

"If you mean did I understate the risks, I would say definitely not, I've done perhaps eighty such assessments in the seven years I have been with this prison. This is only the second time there has been an incident."

"Miss Martin, are you calling murder an incident?"

"Definitely not, I was referring to day pass infractions, the only other one of mine, was due to a heart attack an inmate had when he choked on some Japanese food and an ambulance had to attend."

"So you played no part in aiding the defendant ?"

Mavis looked at Arnie, as he leaned forward. She replied, " Only to the extent that my professional advice was relied upon by the board, along with several other documents and the defendant's entire criminal record. They had a full history of his activities right before them, to look at."

"Did you meet with the defendant between the time that he escaped in the guard's truck and his apprehension by the authorities the following day?"

"I choose to assert my Fifth Amendment right."

"Did you not meet with him at the Day's Inn Motel on the previous afternoon?"

"Again, I choose to assert my Fifth Amendment right not to answer the question."

"Did you have an ongoing affair with the defendant during the time he was incarcerated at New Haven prison?"

"I choose to assert my Fifth Amendment right."

Robert Woods, showing frustration, threw his sheet of questions on his Prosecutor's table. "I have no further need of this witness." He give Mavis a serious look as he shook his head in disbelief.

The Judge adjourned the court for the day.

Ken Harris, was still appearing upbeat, he knew he could counter act the unanswered question that the prosecutor may ask him. He leaned over and whispered in Jill's ear," put me on the stand tomorrow, I'll blow these bastards out of the water."

I don't recommend you taking the stand, Mr. Harris! Think it over, and I'll see you in the morning."

"We're winning, we have them beat, what are you a quitter?"

"There's a time to keep going, Mr. Harris, and there is a time when quitting is in order, this, I believe, is one of those times. It will take more than charm and wit to convince the jury you didn't commit this crime."

"You think I'm guilty, don't you?"

"What I think is irrelevant! The jury is your problem, and right now I think they have already made up their minds."

Ken, sat motionless for a full two minutes. He seemed to be willing to concede his options were limited. "Do it!"

"Do what?"

"Get me a deal!" He looked away.

"I'll get right on it, I'll have something by morning." Jill walked over to Robert Woods's table. My client wants me to talk to you."

"Fine, meet me in my office in fifteen minutes"

CHAPTER 13

Robert Woods was clearing files that had been stacked on his visitors' chairs when , Jill Conrad , tapped on the doorjamb.

"Come in Jill; you don't know how fortunate you are to work only a few cases at a time. I must have forty ongoing files here, it's crazy."

"Well then, perhaps we can lighten your load on this Harris case?"

"The Judge, wants this one to go the distance, it will look good in his reelection flyer."

"Are you saying I should be talking to him? Come on now let the system work! Take something to him, he may surprise you!"

"Not him! I can read him like a book. I hope to be just like him when I grow up!" Woods laughed.

"Heaven forbid, two hanging judges!"

"Anyhow what do you propose we do for Mr. Harris?"

"How about a sentence of fifteen years, with no death penalty?"

"The press and the electorate will be screaming blue murder! Pardon the pun."

"Let them, it's still five months until the elections. They'll have other cases to bitch about by then."

"I'll present it to his honor. Is tomorrow morning just before court be soon enough for an answer?"

"Sure, let the big fella sleep on it!"

"See me at 9.45 in here tomorrow morning."

"Thanks, Robert, I owe you one."

"Don't worry, I'm keeping score. One of these days I'll need a favor from you, and I'll come calling."

"You know I'll do anything to further justice. See you tomorrow."

"Goodnight Jill."

❦

Judge Darling waved Robert enter his office, "I have only ten minutes ,Robert, the wife wants me at a political gathering later."

"Not already?"

It's never too soon to sow some electoral seeds, Robert. By the way you aren't running against me are you?"

"Not at all, Your Honor."

"Good, that puts me in a good mood. I'm putty in your hands. Talk to me."

"Miss Conrad is suggesting 15 years, and of course no death penalty."

"We'll be seen as too light on persons that kill prison guards. That will not make me the darling of the people or the press." He smiled at his play on words. "How else can we work this out so both parties win?"

Robert Woods hesitated, he had solved such a dilemma once before with another Judge. " Do you remember the Gil Sovline case?"

"The guy that had his wife killed in an arranged hit? Whatever happened to that case."

"He's the one. We made a double deal on it."

"What are you driving at?"

"Initially we agreed that Gil would serve life in prison. That made us look tough on crime."

"So, what became of that case?"

"We had an arrangement, that on appeal, the sentence would be reduced to twenty years. But that didn't happen until almost a year later!" So the Judge got his wish and the defendant got his deal."

"So what are you proposing here?"

"I'll tell them we will agree to life now, and they can appeal later, after the elections."

"You dog! I like it." Judge Darling was only planning on one more term, then, it was retirement city for him in Florida.

"I'll be seeing Miss Conrad at 9.45, perhaps we can all go golfing tomorrow afternoon?"

"Don't push it Robert, all the press has to do is to print is a picture of the three of us swinging away on the golf course after pleading out a murder case."

"Just joking, Your Honor."

"I'm not laughing Robert. I have to go now."

Robert Woods give Jill a typed and signed letter of understanding, it called for a sentence recommendation of life in prison, for Ken Harris, without parole. A further requirement was that he would testify against Mavis martin. Then , verbally, he reminded her that Ken could appeal and perhaps suggest her original offer. He winked at her as he pointed to the mid November election date on his wall calendar.

She nodded, no further words were spoken about the arrangement they had just made. "I'll see if Mr. Harris is in agreement with this, she waved the paper at Robert."

Ken was showing nervousness as Miss. Conrad seated herself at the defense table. "She showed him the letter."

"Nice going counselor, all you got was the death penalty reduction. I hope it didn't overwork or strain your brain."

Jill ignored the comment, "It gives us something to work on, now we can appeal the sentence and try for the fifteen years. It's worth a gamble."

"Go and gamble with someone else's life, I can't do the max."

"Do as much as you can, I know we can get it reduced. The prosecutor indicated as much."

"Let him put it in writing then!"

That's not possible, these things take time to work out, the case is too fresh, let it fade into the past, then we have a better chance."

Ken, barked. Well, alright tell the bastards, I'll agree." Jill nodded to Robert, with a thumb up signal.

"What about your being asked to testify against Mavis?"

"That's the least of my worries! That bitch can defend herself all she wants, she put me here, indirectly she's responsible for all this!' He waved his arm in a sweeping motion covering the courtroom setting.

"As you say, Mr. Harris" with that , Woods waved to the bailiff to approach her table, and give him a message for Judge Darling. The bailiff disappeared into the Judge's chamber. Within a couple of minutes they both reappeared. Court was called into session

The Judge scanned the agreement and brought the Courtroom to attention. " Ladies and gentlemen of the Jury, your services will no longer be required. Even though you have not deliberated on a verdict, your presence and service has assisted in bringing this case to a resolution. I thank you all for your participation in this trail. The jury is dismissed , this Court is adjourned."

CHAPTER 14

Mavis Martin met with Arnie Silverman to discuss her options. "Miss Martin, as you know Ken Harris has entered into a plea agreement ."

Yes, do you know what it was?"

"He gets life without parole, and he testifies against you. Do you think he will hurt your case? I need to know every word you exchanged with him before and after the murder, that pertained to Mr. Charles Dumont ."

Mavis thought back. "Before his death, I did say something to the effect that I wished *someone would stick one to him.*"

"What was Ken's reply?"

"He said Chuck would *get what's coming to him,* and to leave it to him, Ken I mean."

"Did you reply to Ken's statement.?"

"I think I nodded, and then got on with Ken's paper work. Believe me I did not seriously ask Ken to murder Chuck."

"That may very well be the case, but those words can be interpreted as a suggestion , or even an authorization, to do just that, after all you and Ken were lovers!

"I'm telling you, there is no way I would consider killing anyone!"

Arnie ignored her "What was discussed when you met him at the Day's Inn Motel, again just tell me the part about Chuck's death, if it was discussed at all.

"Well, yes, it was let's see, I asked him about Chuck, and if Chuck was with him?"

"How did he answer you?"

"He said Chuck was in LA land, and that he wouldn't be bothering me anymore. I asked if he killed Chuck and he said the death was a boating accident. Of course now we know it wasn't. Then I suggested we should report the accident. Again we did not. That was the end of any reference to Chuck."

"Did you leave the motel at that time?"

Mavis shook her head negatively and looked at the floor. "I left later, I'd rather not go there"

"The Prosecutor will, be asking, we have to be prepared with the best possible explanation."

"We had a couple glasses of wine, which I brought, then we made love."

"Jesus, woman, what in the hell motivated you?" Arnie was incredulous "do you get off on that kind of behavior? Partying with a suspected killer!'"

" You weren't there. Are you saying that that visit with him alone will convict me?"

"If Ken brings all that up, then we'll have no alternative but to put you on the stand."

"He, won't say anything, I assure you! I could talk to him."

"I don't share your optimism, in any way, on that point! Besides, both of us are restricted from having any contact with him. We have to wait and see what transpires in court."

"Can we get a plea agreement?"

"Sure if you want to spend the next twenty-five years in prison? You are charged with conspiracy to murder. I see this as an all or nothing case, either we get you off or you can get a twenty-five year subscription to Readers Digest."

Mavis shook at the thought. "You're scaring me?"

"And you should be scared! This is big time, serious stuff. But, enough of this speculation, I will review the Harris trial transcript and prepare the case . I'll be meeting with you a few more times as questions come up and also to prep you."

CHAPTER 15

THE TRIAL of Mavis Martin

Robert Woods, was once again the lead prosecutor in the Mavis Martin trial. The Judge in the case was her Honor Judge Nancy Greer. She had a reputation as an experienced but fair and a *by the book kind of* Judge.

Arnie was pleased that they had been assigned a female Judge, he was somewhat less so about how Judge Greer would view his theatrical performances in the courtroom. He was further pleased with the Jury of eight women and four men, with two alternate men jurors. The mix, leaning toward females, favored Mavis Martin's case.

Woods presented his opening statement, which paralleled the statement he had used for the Harris case.

"YourHonor, Ladies and gentlemen of the jury. The prosecution will clearly show through the evidence collected and the testimony of witnesses and others that on Friday, June 23, 2006 at approximately 9 a.m. the defendant, Miss Mavis Martin, conspired with a prison inmate, Ken Harris, to willfully murder the victim Charles Dumont.

While on a day pass, Mr. Harris and Mr. Dumont were canoeing and fishing on the Ansonia Reservoir. Within less than an hour Mr. Harris allegedly engineered a supposed canoeing accident. Mr. Dumont lost his life. The prosecution will clearly show that Mr. Harris seized that opportunity to take advantage of the mishap, and that he subsequently murdered Mr. Dumont, who was working as the defendant's guardian while Mr. Harris was on a day pass.

Afterwards, Mr. Harris fled the scene, stole the victim's vehicle, and was at large for approximately 24 hours. During that period the defendant Miss Martin, met Mr. Harris in a motel and they partied for approximately two hours. We will show that the defendant knew that she was putting Charles Dumont's life at risk when she approved the pass; furthermore she did nothing to stop Ken Harris from remaining at large. She did this even though she had every opportunity to notify the authorities of their planned motel rendezvous. Her careless acts exposed police and other persons to further possible danger at the hands of Mr. Harris.

The defense will of course mitigate Miss Mavis Martin's participation to that of a poor innocent, woman in love. I intend to prove she was negligent in her professional duties as a prison psychologist and that her actions were instrumental in contributing to Charlie Dumont's death.

Don't be swayed by the defenses explanations, interpretations and twisting of the facts in the case. They will try to build a defense for an indefensible crime, thank you Ladies and Gentleman.

"Mr. Silverman, do you have an opening statement?" Judge Greer had heard of Silverman's tactics from her fellow judges.

"Anything to please the court, your Honor!" Arnie quipped as he stood and took his position facing the jury.

"Ladies and Gentleman of the Jury, the Prosecutor has no case. He is contending that the defendant Miss Martin was conspiring with Mr. Harris to murder Charles Dumont!

As we go through the circumstantial and misinterpreted evidence and testimony of unreliable witnesses, it will be clear to you that the facts themselves will show that my client was not complicit, or in any way responsible for Mr. Dumont's death.

We will show that the circumstances of the death of Mr. Dumont resulted from a freak accident and that Mr. Harris himself, and himself alone took advantage of the situation to make good his escape.

Charges against my client are greatly overstated and unsubstantiated, that in itself should, in your minds, create a reasonable doubt as to her guilt. We look forward to dealing with every piece of evidence and the testimony of the prosecutor's witnesses and experts. In turn the defendant insists that she not only wishes to testify on her own behalf, but that she demanded to he be allowed to do so. Is that the actions of a woman with something to hide? I say not. It is the action of a woman that believes she has been falsely accused of a crime that she did not commit, thank you Ladies and Gentlemen of the jury.

Arnie took his seat, he liked the reaction the jury portrayed in their body language as they had leaned forward in their seats listening intently to his counter arguments, which resulted in a pointed opening statement. He saw them lean back and begin to relax, as though already thinking that this was going to be an easy case to resolve. "I believe, we got them thinking, our way "he confided to Mavis as the Judge adjourned Court ,for lunch.

The Prosecution, again presented the circumstances leading up to the day of the murder, the evidence pertaining to the actual crime and the subsequent of the actions of Ken Harris. Arnie sat without any comment, other then "no questions at this time, we reserve the right to recall the witness" as each witness repeated their original testimony. He made a few notes, but doodled much of the time. He was the perfect picture of a strategist waiting for his opportunity to "Checkmate" his opponent. He stopped his faked inattention when Ken Harris took the stand.

Robert Woods was basking in his easy ride. Little did he know the case was about to head downhill like a runaway toboggan on a New Hampshire ski slope!

"Mr. Harris , would you confirm to the jury your relationship to the defendant Miss Martin."

"She was my shrink in New Haven Prison."

"Is that all?"

"Do you mean personal crap?"

Judge Greer interrupted, " The witness will refrain from using undignified language."

"Sorry your Honor." Ken rephrased his answer. " Mavis and I were close friends."

"Could you elaborate on what you mean by close friends."

"Look at her, she's an attractive woman, and I'm a man."

"Were you sexually involved with the defendant."

"Bingo." Ken sneered.

Again the Judge cautioned the witness. "Mr. Harris, now clearly say yes or no to that last question."

"Yes, a big yes, your Honor!" The courtroom broke out in laughter. The Judge restored order.

Woods continued. "Now Mr. Harris, did the defendant ever discuss murdering Mr. Dumont.?"

Ken hesitated, he looked at Mavis and said, "I'm sorry Honey," then he faced the prosecutor saying, "Once after Chuck was teasing her about our affair, she suggested she would be happy to see him stuck."

"What do you think she meant by stuck?"

"Knifed , I suppose."

Arnie rose "Objection, the witness is not an English Language expert."

"Overruled."

Woods continued." Mr. Harris, what was your response when she said she wished he would be stuck?"

"I said that she should leave it to me. I would deal with Chuck.""

"Did you at that time seriously plan to murder Mr. Dumont?"

"Hell no! I was just talking trash to score some points with Mavis."

"Now let's jump ahead to your motel rendezvous with Miss Martin, after your escape from custody. Was she concerned with Mr. Dumont's absence?"

"Well, she asked where Chuck was. I told him he had an accident and drowned."

"Did she believe you?'

"I doubt it; anyhow we stopped talking about it at that point."

"What did you and her do then?"

"We had some wine, and in about half an hour we were making love."

"No more questions ". Woods nodded toward Arnie.

"Well, I have a few questions of Mr. Harris. Mr. Harris, is your appearance here today the result of a plea arrangement in your own case?"

"You got it!"

"Would you say Miss. Martin's utterance in a moment of frustration was the motivation that resulted in your killing Mr. Dumont."

"Not really!"

"Explain that."

"When I hit the bastard, sorry Judge, when I struck that Chuck guy with the paddle, I just wanted to get away, I didn't want him shooting at me as I was making it to shore."

"So you did not expressly act on orders from Miss. Martin, to kill Mr. Dumont."

"No, I didn't." Ken looked at Mavis, hoping she would see that he was minimizing her involvement."

"Now when you met later in the motel were things pretty much normal?"

"What do you mean, normal? We got it on. If that's normal then yes, things were pretty much normal.""

"Was she her usual self, or was she nervous?"

"She was something; I had to tell her to keep her mind on our lovemaking. Something was bothering her."

"I guess so! " Arnie turned to the Judge, "No more questions of this witness.at this time."

Robert Woods stood forward." Your Honor, that concludes the prosecution's case."

"Court is adjourned until tomorrow morning ."

Arnie met with Mavis to prep her for the following day. "Mavis, after I cross examine Mr. Harris, further, you'll be taking the stand. In your opinion, was there anything that Ken said that was not accurate?"

"No, he actually took it easy on me, on a few points."

"We won't worry about that, was there anything he said that I should ask him to clarify?"

"No, but I'll think about it overnight and let you know."

›

Arnie recalled Ken Harris the next day. "Tell me, Mr. Harris was Miss Martin anywhere near the lake on June 23, 2006?"

"No, she was not."

"Was she involved in the actual killing of Mr. Dumont?"

"No."

"Did she assist you in stealing the vehicle and fleeing?"

"No, of course not!"

"Did she provide you with any credit cards, cash or other aids that helped you make the escape from, custody?"

"No, she knew nothing of what happened until after we met at the motel," Ken shook his head," She did nothing, this is all so much B.S."

"Objection, the witness is expressing an opinion."

"Sustained, strike the last sentence of the witness's response."

"No more questions." Arnie turned to the bailiff, "The defense calls Jim Trent."

"You are the Warden at the New Haven Prison?"

"Yes."

"Do you know Miss Martin, the defendant, and Jim Harris the person convicted in the murder of your guard Charles Dumont."

"Yes, Miss Martin was on staff, and Mr. Harris was an inmate."

Silverman, drew a document from his file, " Do you recognize this form."

"It's the assessment and recommendation that Miss Martin filed on behalf of Ken Harris."

"Is that you initials, approving the form?"

"Yes."

"Could you have used your experience and power as Warden to have the document changed or even halted from being presented to the review board."

"Yes, I have such powers."

"But you did not use them."

"Correct."

"Why not, apparently you told Miss Martin, she was too generous in her wording and recommendations. Is that not so?"

"Yes, I chose to let the report go to the board as it was. I rely on my staff to use their own good judgment?"

"However in this case, you clearly objected to her judgment."

"So, does that make you complicit in the death of Charles Dumont?"

"No, I haven't been advised of any charges against me."

"Don't you find it odd that the buck stopped when charges were laid against Miss Martin?"

"Objection!" Robert Woods interrupted before Trent could answer.

"Withdrawn, I am finished with this witness!" Arnie had scored another point with the jury as Warden Trent slowly and quietly stepped down from the witness box and left the courtroom.

Mavis took the stand. She was conservatively dressed in a grey business suit, a white shirt and black simulated pearl necklace. She appeared apprehensive, as she was sworn in. She took her seat in the witness box.

Arnie approached nearer. "Miss Martin, did you kill Mr. Charles Dumont?"

"Objection!" Robert Woods was on to Arnie's tricks.

"Sustained, it's a fair question. The witness will answer."

"No, I did not." Mavis began to relax.

"Did you conspire with Ken Harris to have Mr. Dumont murdered?"

Mavis shook her head negatively "No, I did not."

"Why are you on trial? Arnie concluded.

"Objection, the Defense is well aware of the reasons."

"Sustained."

"Where were you on the day of June 23, 2006 between 8 a.m. and noon."

"I was at work."

"How far is it from work to the Ansonia Reservoir?"

"I'd guess between 15 and twenty miles."

"You'd need one long paddle to strike Mr. Dumont from that distance!" The courtroom exploded with laughter.

"Objection! Your Honor this is inappropriate questioning."

"Oh, let him have some fun," Judge Greer restored order and ruled, " However, Mr. Woods, I will sustain your objection."

Arnie continued cautiously. "Miss Martin, why did you not notify the Prison authorities when Mr. Harris called and asked you to meet him at the Days Inn Motel?"

"I thought I could talk to him and persuade him to turn himself in?"

"Were you not putting yourself in danger?"

"Ken would not hurt me, he's not that kind of man."

Arnie did not wish to pursue the kind of man Ken Harris was, he already knew.

"Did you actually get to ask him to turn himself in?"

"Yes, indirectly, I suggested we report the drowning accident to the authorities? He ignored my suggestion."

"You took wine to the motel that day at the defendant's request. Why did you do that?"

"I thought it would mellow him out and he would agree to turn himself in."

"Whose idea was it to have sex in the motel?"

"Ken insisted, I let him in spite of my being upset with his behavior."

"When did he leave?"

"About an hour and a half after I arrived there."

"Did you phone the authorities at that time."

"No, I should have, but I was too distraught."

"Are you in love with Ken Harris?"

"I thought I was, now I realize he conned me with his , lies, smile and charm."

"Were you not trained to recognize those tactics in prisoners?"

"Yes, but I was too close to the situation."

"No more questions."

Robert Woods had one question on cross-examination. "Do you feel responsible in any way for the death of Mr. Charles Dumont?"

"I did not kill him or conspire to have him killed."

"You evaded the question, do you feel any responsibility whatsoever." Mavis glanced at Arnie, he nodded to her to answer the question, he had prepped her for just that question.

"I was not totally removed from the situation."

"Can you expand on that?"

"If someone is involved in a car accident because they were at the wrong place at the wrong time are they responsible for the crash, even though they did nothing wrong?"

"I'll ask the questions, Miss Martin. So you admit you were somewhat involved in the death of Charles Dumont?"

"Not any more than Warden Trent, or the Review Board, or Ken Harris's mother, or his teacher in grade school, or anyone who had any interaction with Ken Harris."

"Your Honor, have the witness answer the question put to her."

"You asked your question and you got the witness's answer Mr. Woods, do you have any further questions for this witness?"

"No, further questions, your Honor."

Arnie was beaming as Mavis rejoined him at the defense table. "We got them on our side girl," he whispered as he surveyed the jury members. He stood up, "The defense rests, your Honor."

"We'll hear closing arguments in the morning."

"Robert Woods approached the defense table, " how about a coffee Arnie?"

"Two cream and four sugar, Robbie," Arnie saw a deal in the works. He turned to Mavis, " Miss Martin, I'll be back to you in perhaps an hour, I smell the sweet scent of victory pervading this stale courtroom atmosphere!"

Mavis, smiled for the first time in three months, "You're a sweetheart Arnie." She patted his upper arm and left the courtroom, with a spring in her step.

Arnie joined Robert Woods in the prosecutor's office. A cup of coffee with two creamers , four sugar and a donut awaited him. " Hey, I like the royal treatment!" He exclaimed.

"You earned it, I'm ready to concede the jury bought your arguments." He continued, I'll drop the murder conspiracy charges if your client pleads guilty to breach of trust, agrees to a two year suspended sentence, and loses her license to practice in the state."

"In this State only?"

"Sure, she can go to any adjoining State and reapply there."

"That sounds fair, I'll be back to you in an hour. Now, let me drink my coffee and eat my donut, I want to relish my success. Here have half a donut, you should be rewarded as well, you did a super job in putting Ken Harris away."

"It looks that way, doesn't it?" Robert winked at Arnie. They proceeded to switch their conversation to everyday things like wives, and kids, and sports and international politics

Mavis Martin accepted the plea arrangement and began lecturing at universities on the responsibilities of professionals to their patients, clients and charges.

Ken Harris's appeal for a reduced sentence was rejected by the appeal court, much to the delight of Robert Woods. The con man had been conned. Miss Jill Conrad feigned disgust and contempt for the court system as she dutifully informed Ken Harris of the appeal board's decision.

The End

THE GHOST
LOVERS OF
DOUGLAS LAKE

CHAPTER 1

August 2013

The red canoe glided silently across the still dawn mist-shrouded surface of nondescript Douglas Lake. The occasional early morning sound of a paddle lifting out of the brackish brine and then returning for its' next stroke was the only resonance the lone paddler made.

The craft drifted closer to shore, 200 yards, 150 yards, 125 yards, and 100 yards. Then the paddler witnessed a gray dense human form rise, breaking the surface of the water, it was within several feet of the shore.

The paddler shook his head to ensure he wasn't hallucinating. He wasn't, he looked again, it was still there! The ghostly form advanced onto shore, shrouded, as in a dark dense smoke, up the gentle inclined slope it moved, to higher ground. It shuffled like a heavily laden person, reminding the paddler of a fifty-year-old laborer. The shoulders of the apparition moved in rhythm with the clouded gait of its legs. The paddler's heartbeat made his life jacket vibrate as the craft glided the remaining short distance to shore.

Then the apparition vanished, not like a remnant of a fog patch, which gradually dissipates into less dense vapors as it fades away in the early morning sun. Rather the being, if it was a being, simply vanished in Star Trek fashion in the space of perhaps two seconds.

There was only one explanation, "I've seen a ghost!" Rod Williams exclaimed as the canoe bow, slid up the sandy-muddy shore. He stepped out of the canoe, pulled it up onto shore, and carefully examined the shore area for some sign of telltale footprints. The only visible signs of any fresh disturbance were his own prints and those of his dragged canoe, which he had made a scant 45 minutes earlier. "I've seen an honest to goodness ghost," he repeated, to no one in particular. He peered into the surrounding grove of cottonwoods and willows, he was alone, or was he!

Was the ghost still nearby? He had an eerie feeling that it was. A shiver raced up and down his spine as he, retrieved a camera from his glove compartment, came back down to the lake, and re-launching his canoe, he continued fishing for rainbow trout. Was it a coincidence that on that morning he caught no fish whatsoever? Normally at that time of year, he would have his limit of four fish within two hours. *Was the ghost of Douglas Lake affecting the fish?*

He had heard tales of First Nations people and other local residents in the sparsely populated area mention strange sightings and occurrences. Many of them refused to go out on the lake. Rumor had it that the center was 'bottomless.' That assumption was of course illogical; however, it did reinforce the high regard some people view of the little dangerous lake. The pioneer 'Douglas Family Cemetery' was located a scant one third-mile from the lake. Was there a connection between these numerous unexplained events and the several dozen restless souls interred in boot hill? Were these poor souls searching for their past kin, in the murky depths of Douglas Lake? Did someone drown in the lake, never to be found? Was this ghost the soul of that unfortunate person?"

Rod decided he would research the archives in the neighboring city and obtain an insight into the 140 year history of Douglas lake and its' pioneer families. He discovered several people had died in and near the lake, some in farming accidents, road mishaps, one drowning and one very bizarre gunshot victim, whose common law wife was tried for his murder.

The drowning victim, or so presumed, was in fact nine year old Scott Douglas, son of Joe Douglas. Apparently, Joe went out on the lake every day for months after his son disappeared. Traces of his clothing were found clinging to a homemade raft that the youngster had built out of some old barn logs , wrapped loosely together with barbed wire. "An accident waiting to happen" was the wording in the Coroner's report, in which he concluded the victim was missing and presumed drowned.

An interesting situation, Rod thought. He let his imagination run rampant. Could the apparition he saw that morning be the wandering soul of Joe Douglas, the victim in that shooting 123 years earlier? Was Joe still searching the lake for his son Scott, who had drowned in the lake 130 years earlier?

CHAPTER 2

1889

Joe Douglas, could only be described as a malicious, cantankerous, drunken Son of a Bitch. Joe's main goal in his miserable booze filled life, he was just short of his 50th birthday, was to corner the whiskey market. He proceeded to do this by personally drinking dry every bottle he could lay his grubby hands on. Heaven help anyone or anything that disagreed with him and his drinking habit.

He had not always been like that. In fact, he has made a small fortune in the 1880 Australian Gold Fields, added to it in the Klondike Gold rush, and eventually settled in the small community of Sudden Valley, in central Vancouver Island. In the next twenty odd years he prospered by farming, raising livestock, horses and operating a small illegal still in the back portion of his 160 acres. He was well liked in the community, especially by the women, and he considered himself a 'Ladies' Man'. He danced like there was no tomorrow, and he prided himself on his ability to flirt with women without upsetting their husbands. In short, Joe was everyone's friend. Gradually his drinking obsession changed all that, and his friends became fewer and those that remained kept him at arm's length.

Nevertheless he did appeal to one Mary Jane James who decided to forsake her own husband, Malcolm, and their four children when she succumbed to the questionable charms of 'Whiskey Joe. The fact that they were first cousins had no bearing on their raucous relationship. Joe drank, Mary Jane drank, then they argued. After their arguments, they engaged in mad passionate love, or so they imagined they did while in their drunken stupor. Occasionally they beat on each other: however, Joe with his bodily mass and downright meanness was more often the beater and Mary was the victim.

Because the times regarded adultery as a greater sin than drunkenness or wife beating, Mary yearned to regain her respectability in the community. She gave Joe an ultimatum on Christmas Day 1889. "Marry me you Goddamn pieced of shit, and do it before July 31, of next year, or by Jesus I will kill you." It wasn't the most heartwarming proposal that she could have originated, but it did get Joe's immediate attention.

Taking two quick steps toward her, he wacked her on the right side of her head with a half-full bottle of moonshine whiskey. "Who do you think you are, you two- bit good for nothing, floosy? Didn't I agree to take you in when your husband and that pack of retards, you called your children, give you the boot?" He then proceeded to strike her on the left side of her head so the bruising would be symmetrically pleasing. He hated artwork that did not portray life as it ought to be.

"Just, remember what I said." She groaned back, between flashes of pain. "Give me some of that whiskey before it kills you, I don't want to be cheated out of the pleasure of either marrying you or seeing you dead."

Joe relented, pouring five ounces of gut-rot into a ten-ounce tumbler and handing it to Mary. "I'm sorry I ruffed you up a bit, sweetie." He was now using his most charming tone.

"I know you're a good man, Joe, let's not fight any more tonight, let's celebrate Christmas, you know how much my holidays mean to me." They drank to their good health, they toasted the passing year, the coming New Year and they even toasted their neighbor and his wife, Mr. & Mrs. Mosher. After their many toasts, they rolled into bed and the early evening was spent as usual with moans of pleasure drifting across the lake to the sounds of the children singing "Silent Night" over at the community hall.

Mr. Henry Mosher was the preacher at the local Lutheran Church and of course, his wife Misty Mosher was a little angel that would soon be able to walk on water along with her husband. They had no use for Joe and Mary considering them heathen, unrepentant sinners, adulterers, and most of all irritating people to have as neighbors. That night Reverend Mosher was the M.C and sing a long leader for the forty or so 'Christians' he had saved from damnation during the past years. They pretended not to hear the Douglas /James duo, exciting each other with booming climaxes. Instead, they told the children the sounds animated from a pack of coyotes that were yapping at the moon. Five-year-old Johnny thought otherwise. "That sounds like mommy and daddy did early this morning!" He exclaimed. His mother excused herself along with Johnny, prudently deciding Johnny needed to use the outdoor biffy.

And so, life in the district of Douglas Lake continued. Winter passed, spring sprung, and then changed to mid summer. July 31, was fast approaching and Joe had not even mentioned marriage much less proposed to Mary. She was seething, like a dingo that had been chased off a kill, hadn't she been a dedicated loving companion to Joe for over a year now?"

Mary was not about to let him forget her proposal deadline. It was late afternoon, Joe was out at the haystack searching for a hidden bottle, with his back turned to the barn, when a rifle shot rang out and the fencepost next to him splintered with an immense cracking sound, sending fragments flying as the 30-30 bullet shattered the valley tranquility. Joe swung around with a malicious sneer "What the hell are you doing, Mary? Are you trying to kill me?" As he hollered, he picked up a pitchfork leaning against the barn and ran straight at Mary threatening to spear her to death.

Mary unnerved by her sweetheart rushing toward her, she levered another cartridge into the chamber and raised the rifle to fired once more. Before she could level the rifle and squeeze the trigger, he slammed the barrel of the rifle with his pitchfork, sending the rifle spinning out of Mary's clutch and down unto the ground, where it discharged harmlessly. With a second swing of the fork, he knocked Mary backward and she landed on her fat derriere in the manure pit. The fight was over good-natured Joe saved her from suffocating, by extending the pitchfork so she could balance herself and sit up and pull herself erect. She stepped away from the quagmire of stinking cow manure. That was the final straw, she repeated her ultimatum. "You have two days to do the right thing, Joe, or I promise you right here and now, you are a dead man!"

Joe rather believed she might be serious; however, he was not the type of man that let a woman, any woman, dictate how he would run his life. "Go clean yourself up in the fucking lake, you blue eyed bitch. Forget any notion of me marrying you in two days, or two years, or in two lifetimes. I can have my pick of women up and down this valley. You should be thankful that I don't boot your stinking ass down the road and back to where you came from. You never had it so bloody good, I dare you to find someone better than me who will team up with you and look after you, and your cat, like I do.

"Leave Missy out of this, she's a good cat, a good mouser; she likes you and is deserving of your respect." Mary strolled down to the lake and began disrobing and washing the muck off her body. Watching Mary undressing and cleaning herself was almost too much for Joe. He began going down to the lake to make up with Mary, but then he reminded himself to think long-range smart, and not short range stupid.

He turned and went back to finding his whiskey. He could smooth things over later once he got a shot or two of calming booze into her. *Maybe I should marry her,* he thought, *I could use some ex-cuse to get rid of her later on if someone better comes along.* He knew that she had not been properly divorced from Lloyd James, so mar-rying her would still not make her his legal wife. He would see if she got over her sulking tonight and then he would announce his plans for their marriage.

Under her breath, Mary was steadily cursing Joe for once again hu-miliating her. She just wanted to impress upon him that there were only two days left, before her deadline and she was hoping to jolt him into action. She had gotten action all right, now she was even angrier with Joe then before. He was aware of her desire and the date, and he still refused to bite the bullet. She smiled at her metaphor. She wished she had shot the maniac in the choppers when she fired her first shot. At the time, she was just hoping to scare him into proposing to her. Her scheme backfired, or more correctly, it landed her in more shit. She had it with Joe. She was going to give him one more chance! Tonight she would break out a special bottle of store bought rye whiskey, she had squirrel away just for an occasion like this, lure Joe into the bedroom and try to make a real man out of him once more.

She had another reason to get the marriage bells ringing, she had learned from her doctor just two days before that she was three months into a pregnancy. She had not yet told Joe, she was waiting for the right time to slip the news to him. She feared it would be unwelcome news to Joe and he might become enraged and violent with her. Tonight could be the right moment

Joe's eyes lit up at the sight of Mary, or was it the store bought Whiskey bottle that brought out the sparkle in his eyes? In any event, it was party time and Mary's plan seemed to be working out just as she had planned. The evening turned into a lovemaking night and the night into a lovemaking morning day.

Mary snuggled up to Joe and purred, "Sweetheart, how would you feel if I said you were going to be a daddy?

Joe's reaction was even more severe that Mary had expected. " You fool! You went and got pregnant on purpose, didn't you? You bitch."

"No, honest Joe we just got carried away around Easter, you remember that party we had over at your brother's house. I think that was the night it happened."

Joe's mind jumped to find a possible excuse to extradite himself from any responsibility for the pregnancy." It's that stinking, sneak of a brother Jack that did this to you, isn't it?"

"No, I have never had any feelings for Jack. This is your baby, there's been no one else since we got together. You have to believe me. Why can't you act like a responsible man, for once in your miserable life?"

"Look Mary, there is not going to be any baby, get rid of it, or by God I'll do it for you. Do you hear what I am saying?"

"You want to kill your own child? How cruel can you be?"

"Look I told you it's not my kid! Now listen one more time. Go see that doctor in town I heard he causes miscarriages." Joe got out of bed and got dressed. He began looking for a bottle with some whiskey left in it. He couldn't find any.

Mary had a secret cache, she went to the closet and returned with a half bottle, "Here, Joe, let's have a drink and calm down we can sort this out."

The whisky looked inviting, Joe took the glassful Mary handed him, and downed it in one big gulp. "Fill it up again." She did and again he emptied the glass, "More, give me more, hurry!"

"What about the baby, Joe, what about the baby?"

"Have your Goddamn baby, but don't ever ask me to hold it, I don't hold kids that aren't mine."

"How can you say that! You're heartless, and a bastard to boot."

"You're the one having a bastard. Now give me another drink."

The whiskey had run out. Still no proposal was forthcoming from Joe, apparently replenishing his whiskey ranked above the lesser duty of proposing marriage. "It's all gone Joe."

Joe snorted "Damn it " He put his boots on and went out in the barn, soon he was hitching the two horses to the wagon.

Mary came out and hurried over to the wagon, "Where do you think you're going?"

"I'm going to town to get some more Whiskey!"

"What about my proposal? What about the baby?"

"Stuff them both down a rabbit hole, for all I care."

Mary saw the rifle in the wagon. "Don't take that gun into town."

Joe, lifted it over the edge of the wagon and said "Here take it the house." He winked at her and teased her. "Go ahead pull the trigger

THE GHOST LOVERS OF DOUGLAS LAKE   73 and shoot me dead!" He should have been more careful of what he was saying.

Mary, reached for it , lifted it up on her shoulder in a half military style and turned toward the house. With her back to Joe, the rifle discharged, Mary turned in horror just in time to see Joe tumbled forward and slam head first to the ground, dead! He had been shot in the head. The horses galloped off with the wagon in tow, they went racing up the trail leading out to the main road.

Mary couldn't believe what she had done! Had she killed her sweetheart!

A neighbor, Hugh Dunn, riding by and seeing the runaway horses was able to halt them. He brought them back to the farm. He led them back to where Mary was draped over Joe's body, crying and repeating, 'It was an accident, it was an accident, my Joe is dead."

Hugh checked Joe and determined by the fact that 1/3 of his head was missing that Joe has had his last drink, actually his last anything! He helped Mary up and taking her to the house, he instructed her to wait there until he went the eight miles into town and sent back the authorities and other help for her.

Within two hours, Mary Jane James was placed under arrest and charged with the first-degree murder of the one Joseph Michael Douglas.

Mary Jane James was allowed to be free on bail, pending her trial, which was in its self, an unusual event in 1889. Her estranged children reunited with her on the family farm and assisted her with caring for the livestock and the daily chores pertaining to the farm, while she pondered her future.

Mary Jane experienced a paranormal event while awaiting trial. One month after Joe's death she was awakened just as dawn was breaking by screeching sounds that emanated from the lakeshore, some two hundred yards from the house. She went to the window that faced the lake and saw a ghostly form making its way steadily up the narrow pathway. She recognized it as a manifestation of Joe. The sighting did not frighten her, rather strangely , it made her want to go to him. She grabbed her robe, stepped into a pair of rubber boots laying on the back step and hurried to meet Joe. When she was within fifteen or so feet, the apparition spoke, "Mary Jane, I need you, let's go back in the house." She complied without question and led the way back to the house. She disrobed, climbed back into bed and drew back the covers as though inviting Joe to join her. She closed her eyes, in an effort to show she was ready for love. As she lay there, she felt the presence of Joe's body lowering itself onto her. She felt no weight, which was understandable, but there was that warm sensuous feeling that comes when two lovers unite. For the next thirty minutes, she enjoyed the closeness that she had known on occasion with Joe. Then as suddenly as his apparition had appeared, it left her side and lingered at the end of the bed.

She heard the faintest of whispers, "Mary Jane I forgive you. I know it was an accident."

Then the form dissolved and vanished. Mary Jane had to blink her eyes in disbelief! Had this encounter really happened? She looked down examining her lower body. She hadn't been drinking that evening. Had she dreamt and felt the entire experience as real? The encounter left her feeling mellow and looking forward to dealing with the personal stress her trial would create for her. Now she knew she could relax, after all, it was an accident, even Joe admitted that! She wondered if she would ever again be visited by Joe's ghost. The thought sent goose bumps up and down her spine. She yearned to have that 'cloud nine' experience repeated. She hoped it would happen again, soon, real soon!

The Douglas clan had other ideas, they contended that Mary Jane had no entitlements to the property and possessions of Joe Douglas and they hired a lawyer to commence legal proceedings against Mary Jane, In case she was acquitted of the murder. They learned that if Mary Jane was found guilty, she could not by law, benefit from her crime and would not have any claim whatsoever on her victim's estate.

CHAPTER 3

The trial begins

It was a cold, mist shrouded morning on November 2, 1890, a fitting kind of weather for holding a murder trial. It was especially fitting because of the violent and tumultuous windstorm nature, of the Douglas/James relationship. The small courtroom was packed to capacity, another adjoining room was jammed with witnesses, everyone was prepared to testify in the case, some thought Joe was a pillar in the community. They were right he had been for some ten years until his love affair with the bottle took control of his life.

Others were prepared to attest to his mean, viscous nature when drunk and had witnessed his less than loving acts of cruelty he inflicted on Mary Jane James. Yet others could say what a decent, kind woman Mary Jane James was, and how she was to be admired to put up with the abuse she was subject to at the hands and, literally , the boots of Joe Douglas. The stage was set for a drama-filled trial because of the varying views of the witnesses, as well as, the expert witnesses.

The Judge David Agassiz, came down from nearby Nanaimo, B.C. to preside over what the prosecutor thought would be a five-day trial. The jury of twelve men, were chosen swiftly. The defense looked for only one trait, men that were presently in solid happy marriages. The prosecutor, Harold Fast, was oblivious to the selection process. He felt he had an airtight case and looked past the jury selection process to the day when the trial would conclude with a 'guilty' verdict.

Fast's opening statement was also brief and hastily presented " Gentlemen of the jury, Mary Jane James, the cousin and common law wife of Joseph Michael Douglas did on August 2, 1890, murder the said Joseph Michael Douglas. It was a deliberate act all planned; we will show motive, opportunity and intent. This was no accident, it was a cold deliberate and successful murder plan from start to finish. Don't be swayed by irrelevant claims that the defense will raise in an attempt to minimize the defendant's involvement. The defendant picked up a rife and killed the man that had provided her with all the comforts of life during their cohabitation.

We contend that this unnatural, adulterous relationship was doomed from the start and ended when the defendant in a blindness rage carried out her threat to kill the victim. A threat that she had been verbalizing constantly during the six months prior to the death of Joe Douglas."

Julian Miller, the defense attorney had been more deliberate in preparing his defense for Mary Jane. He knew that the all men jury of the times would be a difficult group to sway toward a not guilty verdict.

His opening statement was pointed, "Gentlemen of the jury, I will prove to you that the death of Joseph Michael Douglas was a case of accidental shooting. It was not premeditated as the Prosecutor contends, and Mary Jane James is not a cold calculating person, rather she was a devoted companion and mentor to the victim and should be commended on her efforts to make a functional household for the two of them."

The coroner was the first witness. "I arrived approximately two hours after the shooting and examined the victim."

"Was he dead at that time?"

"Yes, indeed, a portion of his skull was ten feet away from the body, his brain matter was strewn all along the distance. Yes, I concluded he was about as dead as one can get!" He smiled at his dark reference. The courtroom broke into raucous laughter.

Judge Agassiz, thought otherwise, " The next person that disrupts the court will be ejected." He turned to the Coroner, "And you, sir, can be more technical and less slapstick in your replies."

"Yes, Your Honor."

The prosecutor continued. "Was the rifle that caused the wound, nearby?"

"No, by the time I arrived one of the family members had removed it from the scene and taken it inside the house. He produced it, up at the house, when I requested he do so."

"Was it the murder weapon?"

"It was freshly fired, judging from the smell of gunpowder emanating from the barrel and the action of the rifle."

"Did you turn the weapon over to the Constable that arrived to complete the investigation?"

"Yes, he took charge of the weapon."

"Did it have any more shells in the magazine or chamber?"

"No, it was empty?"

"Had the family member removed any cartridges?"

"I didn't ask?"

"Can you comment on Mrs. James condition?"

"Yes, she was alive?" Again, the courtroom exploded with jeers and claps.

The judge, ignored the noise as it stopped as soon as it started."

"No, more questions." He turned to the defense table, "He's all yours."

Miller, the defense attorney, stood up and walked quickly to the witness box. "I have one question and one only. That question is, did the defendant admit to killing the victim, while in your presence?"

The Coroner hesitated, "No, by golly, she had been taken into the house before I got there. When I questioned her about the shooting her exact words were, he looked down at his notes, then looked up, "She said my sweetheart is dead. What am I going to do without him?"

"Did you press her for a sounder answer?"

"No, she was too distraught and the Constable was waiting to question her as well."

"So, you can't say with certainty that it was Mary James that shot Joe Douglas?"

"If certainty is 100% then I'd have to say no, if certainty is 90% or less then I would say she probably did shoot him?"

"Could you determine if it was accidental or deliberate?"

"It could have been either, I wasn't there and my E.S.P. wasn't functioning?" The court buzzed again, the judge smiled slightly, *why not have a little fun while convicting someone?*

"No more questions, for this witness."

Constable Smith was next, he was a different breed of cat, serious, straight faces and completely humorless. He was asked by the Prosecutor to give his statement of events.

"Ten a.m., August 2, 1890,I arrived at the Douglas lake farm of Joe Douglas and found him lying fifty yards from the house, he was dead, and had been for some time. It appeared he had been shot, there was no weapon visible nearby. Ten fifteen, I went in the house and waited for the Coroner to end his conversation with the victim's companion Mary Jane James."

"I began questioning her about the apparent shooting and death of her companion. She admitted that a rifle she had just taken from the deceased had accidently discharged while in her possession. "It was an accident "she said she did not mean to shoot him. I examined a rifle produced to the Coroner and it appeared to have been recently fired. I took it as evidence and talked to several other family members. Several informed me that Mrs. James had threatened the victim many times and that she had taken pot shots at him on at least two recent occasions. I placed Mrs. James under arrest, and we went back to town. I locked her up in the jail cells, and completed my report."

The prosecutor was pleased with the testimony," No further questions?"

Fast had another "I have one question at this time. If the rifle was fired say two days before, was it possible it hadn't been fired on that particular day?"

"If it wasn't cleaned, yes, it is theoretically possible that it was not the murder weapon. However, the defendant admitted a rifle in her possession discharged. A bullet from a rifle killed her companion. "

"But, I suggest that perhaps the bullet came from some other rifle?"

"The point is mute, Sir, if you throw a baseball at my face, and a baseball hits my face, chances are it is the baseball you threw an instant before that hit my face!"

"We aren't playing baseball here are we?"

'Quite correct, Sir, this is murder much more important!"

Miller decided to cut his losses and dismissed the Constable.

Judge Agassiz, was hungry, "The witness will step down. This Court is adjourned until 2 p.m."

CHAPTER 4

The Prosecution continued calling witness after witness testifying to support his contention that the motive for Mary Jane to commit the murder was a strong one. It was Joe's reluctance to marry her by the date of July 31.

That together with the two occasions during which she fired shots at Joe, seemed to be convincing the jury that there was no doubt about the shooting, it was anything but an accident.

Miller, didn't challenge any of the testimony. He wanted those witnesses favoring 'good old Joe' to be processed and done with. He had a list of witnesses and personal character testimonies that would, in his opinion, counteract the damage done by the 'Douglas Sympathizers'.

Miller's first defense lead was to explain clearly to the Jury the difference between murder and manslaughter. He made a favorable impression on both the Jury and the general spectators.

His first witness was a neighboring farmer, Fred Clark, who, Fast, knew would give a balanced account of the Douglas/James relationship. "Mr. Clark give us your impression of Joe Douglas during the last four years."

"Joe was a good fellow when sober; however, when drunk, he was a brute and a bully."

"Can you recount any incidents that you actually witnessed that support your remark?"

"Yes, several, I saw Joe kick Mary Jane in the ribs, with his steel toe boots. On another occasion, we were drinking in the kitchen, and when she refused to get another bottle from the stash of whiskey in the barn, Joe grabbed her arm and twisted it to the extent that she suffered a broken arm. On still another occasion Mary Jane had a black eye and a cut on her head, again at that time I did not see how she received those injuries."

"Did you witness any incident where Mary Jane used physical violence against Joe?"

"No, just verbal threats, when they were arguing, I did hear about the 'pot shot' incidents but I was not a witness to those."

"What else did you know about Mary Jane?"

"She was a hard worker, I saw her out in the hayfield working alongside Joe. I saw her plowing the fields with oxen on several occasions. In addition, the household duties, she tended to the barn chores, cared for the sick animals, assisted in the birthing of the calves. Mary Jane, cared for a large garden and the orchard. She was a capable and knowledgeable farm worker."

"Would you say she was an equal factor in the operation of the Douglas farming activities.

"Yes, much more than equal, almost three quarters of the work was done by Mary Jane."

"No more questions."

Fast, thought he should redirect a few questions to minimize Fred Clark's testimony. " When you witnessed those acts of aggression of Joe Douglas against Mrs. James, would you say there was any provocation on Mary Jane's part, which triggered the violence?"

"Well, in the first instance, the kicking one, she called him a useless piece of garbage, when he refused to take her to the local barn dance."

"An in the second instance when she broke her arm, did she say anything else when Joe asked her to get more whiskey?"

"She just said that he had had enough to drink for the day and that she was sick of his constant drinking and laziness."

"Did you witness Mary Jane's drinking habits?"

"Yes, she liked her drink."

"Did her demeanor change when she drank?"

"Yes, she would get sullen."

"Did she bring up her disappointment with Joe refusing to marry her, when she drank?"

"Yes, that was her obsession to marry Joe."

"No more questions."

Miller called the defendant Mary Jane James to the stand. He began with innocuous questions "Mrs. James, tell the court in your own words, how did you become acquainted with, Joe Douglas?"

"We were cousins and I knew him from the age of thirteen on, Joe had been away for some twenty years, in Australia. When returned from the gold fields in the Yukon he settled on a farm approximately two miles from us. My husband and I had him over for dinner and card games and my kids grew fond of him. They even called him 'Uncle Joe'. After a year or so, my husband, Malcolm, took a logging job up the coast in the winter months. It was during that time that Joe came over quite frequently and helped me and the kids with farm work that needed tending to. Well in short, order we became rather close and when my husband returned and learned from the kids and neighborhood rumors that Joe and I had become lovers. He demanded that I leave. Joe was kind enough to offer me the cottage, next to his house. In return I assumed the duties as his housewife and companion."

"Was the subject of marriage ever discussed?"

"No, not at the time, I thought Malcolm might reconsider and ask me back. After a time, it was obvious that was not going to happen."

"What did you do then."

"The relationship with Joe was going quite well, so I began thinking of getting a divorce from Malcolm and marrying Joe."

"What did Joe think of that?"

"He was happy to have things remain the same as they were."

"Did that upset you?"

"Not at first, I thought he just needed time to get accustomed to the idea."

"Did he?"

"No, after we were together about a year, he began drinking

heavily and we would have disagreements about his drinking. I asked him to stop all the drinking and agree to marry me so we could have proper marriage status, and not be regarded as adulterers by the people we knew."

"Did he agree."

"No, the more I pressured him the more he drank and the more adamant he got that it would not happen."

"Did that bother you?"

"Of course, it drove me crazy, we had everything going for us and marriage would have solved our differences. Finally I give him an ultimatum to agree to marry me by July 31."

"And he didn't did he?"

"No, he refused to discuss it at all."

"Did that anger you?

"Frustrated me, more than angered me?"

"We've heard testimony you threatened to kill Joe, and even took potshots at him, is that so?"

"I didn't mean a word, it was just a ploy to get his attention."

"Even the shots you took at him?"

"Sure, I could have killed him anytime, if that was my intention. I wanted him to take me seriously."

"What about the shot that killed him?"

"That was a complete accident; I took the rifle from him so he wouldn't get into trouble in town with a loaded gun. When I turned to go back in the house, I had the rifle slung over my left shoulder , my hand was on the grip, the rifle discharged and Joe was killed. It was a freak accident. Tell me why would I kill the man I loved and wished to marry?"

"That's a good question, why would you?"

"I wouldn't, it's that simple. Look at me now, I'm up here defending myself, I will be without a companion, I may lose the home I live in, I'm an adulteress, and I have no prospects other than going to prison and perhaps being hung. Is that something a person would deliberately bring on to themselves?"

"No Further questions."

Fast, was literally licking his lips as he stepped forward. "You described yourself as an adulteress did you?"

"Yes, but that is not why I am here, that is a Holy sin, not a criminal act?"

"But murder is?"

"There was no murder, it was an accident!"

"You run out into the yard toward your companion, you're in a drunken rage, you take a rifle from him and within a minute or two he's shot dead, and you're holding a smoking gun, some accident!"

"Objection, the prosecutor is expressing an opinion."

"Sustained, the jury will disregard the last two words. You know better than that Mr. Fast."

"I apologize to the Court." He turned back to face Mary Jane, "Were you drunk when you were involved in this shooting?"

"Shooting accident! I had a few drinks, not many, I was hoping to reason with Joe about going into town so early in the morning."

"So you were extremely angry. Were you?"

"More like annoyed, we could have managed nicely without another drink."

"I put to you, Mrs. James, that you were extremely angry and in a rage because the deadline marriage proposal that he ignored was past, and you deliberately went out there with the sole intention of killing him."

"No, I was just concerned with his safety, I did not want him to hurt himself."

"But, he's dead!"

"It just happened."

"You wanted him dead and it just happened?"

"Objection, the prosecutor is badgering the witness. His questions have been answered."

"Objection sustained, change your line of questioning Mr. Fast."

"No more questions, your Honor."

We'll have closing arguments tomorrow. Court is adjourned."

CHAPTER 5

Mary Jane James, had a short conversation with Miller. "How do things look Counselor?"

"I'd say we scored some points here. There isn't anyone able to say it was not an accident. Like you testified, what good did his death do you? None! Go home and don't discuss the case with anyone, In fact, tell your sons to spend the night elsewhere. You have to have complete rest. And for heaven's sake do not have any alcoholic drink! I want you looking fresh and clear in the morning."

"I'll have a late bath and relax in bed with a novel, I started a few days ago.'

"May I enquire as to the name of the novel?"

"It's Wilkie Collins' *Woman In White,* one of the first murder mysteries ever written."

"I've heard about it, but have not read it."

"I'll be done in a day or two; I'll bring it over to you. It has an intriguing plot, which I will not reveal, as you want to enjoy the build up."

Mary Jane arrived home, did some chores, sent her sons packing, made an omelet and relaxed in her night frock, reading by the light of the kerosene lamp. She was completely intrigued with her novel that was detailing the plan to switch identities between two women so the villain could claim that a rich woman died and then they could inherit her estate. It was nearing midnight when she had an eerie feeling. Glancing up from her novel she again saw the apparition of Joe Michel Douglas. His appearance prompted her to speak "Joe what are you doing here?"

"I just want to see you one more time, honeybunch."

"I miss you Joe, how I wish you hadn't died."

"It's not that bad, I've stopped drinking, and have plenty of time to reflect on how I mistreated you and your kids."

"You did the best you could, Joe. It was the whiskey that made you mean."

"Like I said I won't be coming back any more, I have to move on."

"Tomorrow is the verdict, don't you want to know how my trial will turn out?"

"I would like that, yes, that would be a fitting end, I hope it is ruled an accident, we both know it was just an accident."

"Then come back tomorrow night, if I'm found innocent, I'll be here waiting for you. If I'm not here then you know I was found guilty and you can go on your way. If they hang me, wait for me on the other side and we can be together again. Can your do that?"

"I'll try, maybe I can come one more time?"

"Here Joe," she pulled the covers back, come and hold me just for a few minutes. It would mean so much to me to know you will be mine after all."

"I want to, Mary Jane, but I better go now so I can arrange to come back tomorrow. Can you wait until tomorrow?"

"For you, I'll wait forever, I'll see you tomorrow Joe." The apparition vanished with a swish that sent the flame in the lamp into frenzy. Mary Jane for the first time in twenty years said her prayers and blew out the flame on the lamp. She had every reason to be optimistic about the morrow. Through the window, she could see the full moon streaming down on the still waters of Douglas lake. Everything was in harmony with nature.

CHAPTER 6

Summations and verdict

Defense attorney, Miller, saw a perky Mary Jane as she joined him at the witness table. He cautioned her, "Mary Jane you have to be prepared for any kind of verdict, we won't know for certain until all the Jurors have their say behind those closed doors."

"I know and I don't care, will I be able to spend tonight a free woman? I can't be locked up, not tonight!"

"Why, have you got a date?" Miller chuckled.

"Sort of, I'll tell you after the verdict is in. Will I be able to spend tonight at home?"

"I would expect so, once the verdict is in, the Judge usually leaves sentencing for a day or two. If you are acquitted, then you will be free to leave." Miller was somewhat puzzled by Mary Jane's attitude, to him it appeared that *she did not care whether the verdict was for or against her. Most defendants are on pins and needles, she just wants another day of freedom. He wondered whether it was his duty as an officer of the court to speak to the authorities? What could he tell them? He had a hunch that Mary Jane was planning something, but what? He would look like a fool. He though it best to keep his hunches to himself. He would observe Mary Jane throughout the day, and see if there were any further signs indicating what her plan was.*

Court was called into session, Miller rose to give his summation. "Gentlemen of the jury, thank you for your attention and patience in this matter. I will summarize the case as I see it and show you that there are numerous inconsistencies in the Prosecutor's case against Mrs. Mary Jane James. Firstly, the defendant has maintained throughout the case that it was an accident. The first witness that found her draped over the deceased's body testified so, the Coroner also was informed by her , the Constable and the defendant herself give you an account while under oath to tell the truth. The prosecutor has failed to prove otherwise. That Gentleman creates what the law calls, *a reasonable doubt*, if you concur then you must acquit the defendant just on that fact.

Other information has shown that the defendant was in an adulteress relationship with the victim. That is not evidence of murder. You may not agree with her moral judgment, and many of the people in this room share your that feeling. However, it has to be put aside, it had not bearing on the victim's demise. Actually it is a sign of love, so I repeat, don't put any weight on that fact. Also take into consideration that Mary James is sitting here in this courtroom seven months pregnant. Would any woman in her right mind deliberately kill the father of her own child?

Other witnesses stated she had taken pot shots at the victim. Others testified that she was enraged when he failed to agree to marriage. She did this over a twelve-month period, surely, if she had been serious she would have killed him within the first or second attempt. I my opinion these facts prove that she had no intention of killing him, they were the act of a woman in love who was driven to theatrics and unusual tactics to get her point across so the victim would do the right thing and marry her. If she had indeed wanted to kill him she could have easily done it when he was in a drunken stupor from his heavy drinking.

This whole case is built on a foundation of sand, actually not even sand, but mere speculation. I say there is only one verdict possible, and that is to find the defendant not guilty of all charges. Thank you Gentlemen."

Fast was showing some nervousness as he started his final summation, he could sense that the quietness of the courtroom was a problem he had to overcome by discounting the defense's summation.

"Gentlemen of the jury, a man is dead, he was killed by a rifle that we have proven was in the hands of the defendant when it discharged and killed Joe Michael Douglas. That is murder, pure and simple.

The defense stated that no one witnessed the killing and therefore we can't prove that it was not an accident. I'll tell you right now statistics show that 90 % of murders are not, I repeat, not committed in front of witnesses. What murderer invites an audience to a planned killing? It is plain from supporting testimony that there victim and the defendant had an ongoing difference of opinion of the question of marriage, and the actions by the defendant of shooting and threatening death, and the missed deadline all drove her to decide enough is enough and she elected to follow him out to the yard and kill him. Murder is never pleasant, and a murder that does not receive justice is not acceptable. What if tomorrow you or I for that matter are murdered,? Would we want the murderer to be set free, not likely! Our family would demand justice. That is what I am asking you to dispense. Let the victims family feel that the court system, that we all fought to have a right to, is fair and find Mrs. Mary Jane James, guilty of murder! Thank you for your attention and hard work." The courtroom was again silenced, everyone was looking toward the defendant. Mrs. James was quietly crying into a white silk handkerchief, Miller her attorney was scanning the jury, hoping that a last moment of eye contact with them would remind them of his forceful summation earlier."

The Judge give his final instructions. "The jury is asked to retire to consider and agree on a verdict. Court is adjourned."

It was eleven o'clock, it was quite probable that a verdict could be arrived at before four p.m.

At two o'clock, the foreman asked the judge if they could find the defendant guilty of using a weapon without due care and attention.

The judge informed them that since that the charges on which the victim was on trial for were either capital murder in the first degree or the lesser charge of manslaughter. If they could not agree on one of those, then they were to find the defendant not guilty of all charges.

An hour later, they returned with their verdict. The judge demanded quiet in the courtroom. "Mr. Foreman, has the Jury arrived at a verdict?'

"Yes, Your Honor", the bailiff took the folded verdict from the foreman and handed it to the judge.

"On the charge of capital murder, how do you find?"

"Not guilty!" The courtroom exploded.

The judge restored order. "And on the charge of manslaughter, how does the jury find?"

"Not guilty!" Cheers and boo's filled the courtroom simultaneously. Mary Jane, slumped in her chair, relieved that she had been vindicated, yet saddened that except for two of her sons in the courtroom, she was alone. She turned to Miller. 'I want to thank you for the faith you showed in taking this case."

The judge motioned the defense and the defendant to rise. "Mrs. Mary Jane James, you have been found not guilty of all charges, you are free to go." He was relieved he was a strict judge, but sentencing a pregnant woman to prison or perhaps to the gallows was beyond his idea of justice.

Miller turned to Mary Jane, "The law has prevailed, and you are vindicated, I wish you every success and good fortune. Should you require any further legal services, please feel free to call upon me." He was of course eyeing the asset entitlements legalities that she would be facing at the action of the remaining Douglas's.

"Will you marry me? " Mary Jane smiled at the starlet look on Miller's face. "Hey, counselor, relax, I'm joking!"

CHAPTER 7

Love triumphs

Mary Jane had only one thought as she left Miller's legal office, where she had settled her account.

"Off to your date are you?" Miller winked and smiled. "It must be a terrific feeling to be free of all those accusations and charges."

"Life was better, with Joe." She looked Miller, sullenly in the face and continued. "I will be better after tonight." She didn't elaborate.

As she left, Miller was still shaking his head incredulously. *Here was a free woman and she couldn't wait to return home to a lonely farmstead that held only painful memories for* her.

Mary Jane arrived home just after six that evening. She did the chores and retired to have a meager supper of cold roast and bread, she was not interested in a large meal. She thought about her rendezvous with Joe's apparition later that night. Surely, he would not let her down, they had a joyous event to celebrate, the bedroom would be swinging tonight. She had a bath in the round galvanized tub, that her and Joe trotted out every Saturday evening. After heating up two pails of water, she luxuriated in the warm soapy suds for a full hour.

Stepping out of her bath, she dried off, reached into her wardrobe cabinet, and lifted down a gray box from the top shelf. Opening it up she removed the garment and give it a resounding shake, it unraveled and she held the white never worn wedding dress up to her bosom and admired the delicate intricate lacy handwork that adorned the upper body of the gown. She slipped it on and because of her pregnancy it felt tighter than a year ago when she had first purchased it; however, with some adjustments, it was not tight to the point of being uncomfortable, so she finished dressing and waited by her bed as the clock slowly, ever so slowly move it's hands toward midnight. She read the final six chapters of 'Woman In White', and thought about how she liked the ending.

She then decided to lay down for a short nap. She would need all her energy to entertain Joe when he came. Before doing so, she went to the window and looked along the pathway down to the lake. Other than seeing a beaver swimming across the upper part of the lake, in the moonlight, she saw no other movement.

She awoke with a start, the wick in her coal oil lamp was almost burnt down to the point of extinguishing itself. She knew the time was well after midnight, she went into the kitchen and checked the clock, it was 4.30 a.m.. What had kept Joe? Had he been here and left when he saw her fast asleep? Was he not able to arrange their rendezvous? Would he ever come again? The thought of not ever seeing him made her sad. Why couldn't they have had a final night together? Was that asking too much? Who was deciding these things?

Strolling out into the early November night she, found herself being drawn down the pathway to the lakeshore. She had resistance, she took one step, two, a hundred then a few more. Mary Jane was at the edge of the lake. She gazed into the darkness, her eyes finally adjusted to the pale moonlight. As she scanned the surface of the lake, she heard a swishing sound to her right, *oh that damn beaver is at it again*, she thought. She heard the swishing sound again, this time it came from her right. *How could that be? Are there two beavers?" Then the lake surface a scant fifteen feet directly in front of her swirled in whirlpool fashion., The waters churned a frothy white. There was Joe, standing in three feet of water. He looked like she remembered him when he was in his thirties, black hair, shiny white smile, black bushy eyebrows, and the sexiest voice that she had ever heard. He beckoned to her* Come with me dearest. We only have a few minutes until daybreak. Let's make the most of it."

"Oh, Joe, my love, that is my desire" she took a few steps into the water.

"Here, I'll carry you." Joe advanced toward her and swept her up into his arms. They kissed and kissed again, as he walked backward, "You look like an angel" he whispered as they slowly but steadily drifted out into the lake.

"Can we be together forever?" She answered him.

Yes, forever and more, will you marry me?"

"When?"

"Tonight, now!"

"Oh Joe! Yes, of course, I accept, I will marry you tonight."

Clinging to each other, they drifted out into the middle of Douglas Lake. Happily in love.

The End.

MAYDAY LOVE

CHAPTER 1

The foghorn on the ill-fated ferry, Northern Cross, was crying for attention, as it plied the North Pacific waters just south of the Alaskan Panhandle. The three hundred forty foot ferry was journeying down the Inside Passage a distance of one hundred and sixty miles. On board were ninety cars, and one hundred and twenty-eight passengers. It was just after midnight on a cold October night.

Captain Richard Shelby and his First Mate Becky Morris had other things on their mind. Naughty things.

"Take me; take me now," Becky teased as their lovemaking reached the point of no return. It was destined to rocket straight ahead on in direction that they both desired. Not only desired, but one they had to have, and have now, not later.

Captain Shelby set the vessel's autopilot and turned to Becky. "Coming hard to starboard," Captain Shelby matched her fire. He was only, too pleased to comply. It had been three months since they had broken up over a minor matter. They had not served together since that day, shortly after Christmas in 2010. Now after staff reassignments they found themselves together on the same ship. This now give them their opportunity to reignite a once blazing hot romance.

Their clothes lay strewn in scattered piles around the wheelhouse floor. The vessel was on autopilot and still sounding its' programed fog warning every two minutes. It was wrong, and it was dangerous, however, for the two seasoned lovers it was a daring adventure into a zone of contentment that only two lovers can enter.

Suddenly the vessel lurched violently, as it crashed into and struck an underwater reef, near a tree-loaded Island. The vessel made a forty-five degree turn, not out into the channel, but rather further onto the reef that had grabbed it in the first impaction. The vessel listed to starboard at a thirty-degree angle. The vehicles on the car deck slid down the oil covered, tilting deck and unbalanced the vessel even more as it listed to starboard.

In the space of ninety minutes, what had been a routine passage, had transformed into a dreadful nightmare. The vessel was taking on water, passengers in the cafeteria on the passenger deck had been unexpectedly bombarded with soups spilling over from their sliding bowls; coffee and other beverages spilled and splattered on passengers along with flying cutlery and food laden plates.

The love makers lost interest in their precious moment together as they were yanked apart as though there had been Devine Intervention in their intimacy.

"Becky, what the hell did we slam into?" was Captain Shelby's reaction, as he tried reaching about to gather his clothes, get to his feet and began dressing.

Becky was likewise occupied, reaching up with her two hands and adjusting her tunic upward, as she tried to maintain her balance. "This is not good!"

Her comment was an understatement; the vessel was sinking, sinking fast. The only saving grace, if that was the proper word to use, was the fact that only half the ship was below sea level, as it lay almost on its side on the unforgiving reef.

"Mayday, mayday" was the message the Coast Guard Station operator heard, in the small native village, of Quitsinning, about half a mile from the disabled vessel. Peering out into the darkness several couples walking home from a dance party heard the grinding and loud noises, emanating across the water, when the vessel slammed into the reef.

Recognizing at once the seriousness of such sounds, they ran to their fishing trawlers and other watercraft and started up their boats. Gingerly they set out toward the sound of the foghorn that was still blaring away. In about twenty minutes, they reached the stricken vessel and with the help of the terrified ferry workers, they stretched a rope ladder from the ferry down to the deck of the first fishing boat. They then began helping the ship's passengers transfer down to safety.

Among the first were Captain Shelby and Becky, the first mate. Captain Shelby attempting to assumed command, turned to the owner of the fishing vessel." How many people will your craft here hold?"

"It should be good for at least forty. There are two more boats behind me, between the three of us we can get everyone off."

Captain Shelby, seeing he was ineffective, excused himself. "I'll help with the first-aid duties." He went to the makeshift area where other staff members were directing injured passengers.

The fishing boat owners found it astounding that the captain and first mate had been amongst the first ones off the sinking vessel. "I suppose it's no longer a tradition to go down with your ship, if you're the Captain." One owner remarked as he watched the duo walk away.

Another remarked, "Someone will have Hell to pay over this, that channel is plenty wide to navigate, even in the fog. I wouldn't want to be in his blinking shoes." He said, referring to Captain Selby. "These jerks let their command go to their heads."

"As well as other parts of their anatomy," another commented as he pointed to the Captain's feet that had a sock on one foot and barefoot on the other. Becky's hair was a tussled mess; her lipstick was smeared around like a zombie in a 1945 movie.

Within three hours, all the passengers that could be located were taken ashore and housed in the Questioning community hall. The task of comparing passenger lists with survivors began. It continued into the early morning hours. The final tally was 120 passengers accounted for, eight were missing.

The officials hoped that perhaps some of the missing had made it to the nearby shore of the island and were huddled in the depths of the rainforest.

A contingent of search and rescue personnel were dispatched to the area with orders to conduct a thorough search for people and or debris that might provide further information on what happened to the missing. After two hours they returned, they had two bodies, and two shivering survivors, no other signs of survivors were seen along the sandy beach.

A dive team began preparing to search the ferry, which was now submerged in 200 feet of water. Once it became day light it was deemed stable enough to send down the divers. It was a slow, arduous task, as cars were jammed together, in the murky semi-darkness of the lower car deck. Gradually, with powerful lights, carried by the dive team, they searched each car. After 2 shifts of dive teams and four hours of time, the remaining four bodies were located. It was a young family of two adults and two young children. They obviously had chosen to spend the night in their car rather than in a costly stateroom.

CHAPTER 2

Captain Shelby and Becky Morris, met in the jammed breakfast dining room just after 9 a.m. Shelby asked. "Have you spoken to anyone yet?"

Becky shook her head negatively, "No I have an appointment with the Police investigator at eleven."

"I have to see him at 10.30, look Becky we have to agree on the facts of what we were doing before the ship hit those rocks."

"Richard, you damn well know what we were doing! How can we say otherwise?"

"I mean we have to minimize it so we aren't charged with negligent homicide!"

"Homicide! That's murder! They can't do that, can they?"

"Yes they can if they prove we were careless in out duties on the bridge."

"You're scaring me Richard," Becky looked around to see if they were attracting attention, then she said in a whisper. "Perhaps we should meet in my room in half an hour?"

Richard Selby nodded in agreement "Okay, I'll see you there, right now let's stay separated, so it appears like we are just two random workers from the ship." Becky indicated agreement, and stepped up, and joining the line for the cafeteria buffet. Richard held back for a few minutes.

Half an hour later they were alone in the room, Selby attempted to hug Becky, "Cut it out Richard! " She was feeling agitated, "We're in this bloody mess because of your fucking stupid idea of a good time!"

"I didn't see you stopping me, Becky." Richard stepped back, "now let's forget that part. In fact I say let's forget it for good."

"Do you mean we should lie?"

"Well no, let's not lie, but we can be very tight lipped. Just answer questions in a very general non-self incriminating way. No one saw us, so it doesn't have to come out. For all we know we forgot everything that night, we can't remember a thing, we have complete memory loss"

"Don't be stupid Richard, how can two people both have memory loss? That's absurd." She began shaking, "I'm scared, and I might slip up."

"Look Becky, answer all the questions except the one that asks what exactly you were doing?"

"I can't, I'll just refuse to answer any question of any sort. I can do that, can't I?"

"Of course, well if you take that approach then I will follow your lead. They can speculate until spring comes, they cannot prove a thing against us."

"Then we are agreed, keep mum on everything."

"As I see it, it's the only way to avoid charges against us."

Richard was first the first to be interrogated. He acknowledged he was the Captain that he was on duty on the brig, and was there when the crash occurred. He declined to answer any further questions.

Becky followed and did likewise. The Corporal taking the statements made a note to the effect the two were obvious concealing some facts.

CHAPTER 3

"How did the enquiry go today?" Wanda, Captain Selby's wife wished to know.

In an irritated tone, Richard snapped back, "I don't want to talk about it!"

"Well, you had better want to! The kids came home from school with rumors about you and Becky. Is that the Becky you invited to our Christmas party last year?"

"Yes, she works with me. It's quite normal to invite staff and friends to parties. Since when did you start believing in rumors?""

"Ones like these made me a believer. What bothers me is what else are the two of you up to? I'm beginning to get the wrong vibes from you. Tell me ,are you and Miss wonderful having parties and not inviting me?"

"I would be glad to invite you, but there are no parties. There's nothing going on, we're friends and co-workers, that's all! Are you going to pick my friends for me?"

"Friends, like you and that Linda Cunningham, two years ago? That was a friendship to cherish!"

"No, not like Linda, that bitch had no right telling you lies about her and me!"

"Like that weekend in Vegas with Linda? When you told me you had to work."

"She paid her own way; we happened to coincidently meet in Vegas."

"We've gone over that mister! Look at me, Richard. Do I look like a fool?" Wanda was within four feet of Richards face. "I didn't go to Harvard, but I can determine that the odds of you accidently bumping into Linda in Vegas would be like 50,000 to 1. Now stop your Goddamn lying; it's only upsetting me."

Richard stepped back, "No, you don't look like a fool, you're just acting like one. Now, stop working yourself into frenzy." He turned to walk away.

"You haven't seen me frenzying yet, now tell me are you and this Becky bitch getting it on?"

Richard turned back to face her. "I'm through talking to you; your insulting tone doesn't help. I'm going out. In the mean time, calm down and get over the fact I have some friends down at work," Richard slammed the door as he left.

CHAPTER 4

Captain Selby drove across town to Becky's apartment. She was in and she was alone. "Come up Richard," He took the elevator to the third floor. "Come in Honey, I've been expecting you."

"What do you mean?"

"Wanda phoned me and ranted on and on about you and I having an affair. I guess your daughter heard the gossip around the high school."

"What can we do about it?"

"Nothing let me fix you a drink." Becky made a double rom & coke and handed it to Richard. "You're welcome to spend the night here."

"Is that wise, after our court embarrassment today?"

"We can't turn the clock back. What we do in the privacy of my apartment is our business, no one else's."

"There is still that perception of irresponsibility, I don't like it. Now we find ourselves suspended, from work. We are on trial. And now you want to add fuel to the blazing fire?"

"Why did you come?"

"I just wanted a quiet place to unwind; arguing with Wanda was not doing either of us any good."

"You still love her, don't you?"

"I owe her loyalty; after all we've been married 25 years?"

"What about us, we've been close for 10 years now, don't you owe me anything?"

"Of course, I do Honey! It's a dilemma, I can't win. I'm going to lose my family, or I'm going to lose you. Either way we all lose."

"So, just what are you saying?"

"Let things calm down until the trial is over?"

"Honey, that won't solve anything?" Becky moved closer to Richard.

"It will if we end up serving time." He put his right arm around her and drew her near.

"How can we?" She kissed him and snuggled up against him. "No one knows what went on in the wheel house." She kissed him again.

"We do." Richard led her to the sofa and they sank down into its softness.

"But we aren't talking, are we?" She undid the buttons on her blouse.

"No, but some evidence may come in that will nail us good." Richard had trouble keeping his mind on the topic. He reached under her blouse and undid Becky's front fastening bra. "Let's just keep things clandestine for a couple of weeks until the trial is finished." They slowly proceeded undressing as they got more and more into advanced lovemaking.

"Can I see you, every day or so?" Her breasts began heaving as he pressed his body down unto hers and they began to move in unison.

"Whenever you want, but no going to Vegas." He quickened his movements.

Becky, did not respond, she put her palms on his chest and began pushing Richard away.

Puzzled he asked, "You stopped, what's wrong Becky?" He tried to reestablish their closeness by pressing removing her arms.

"I can't! Now get off me! Get off me now!" She gave him a hard shove, forcing him to withdraw.

"What the hell is the matter with you, Becky?"

"I see a family of four, watching us!"

"Impossible, the drapes are drawn, there's no one anywhere here."

"In my mind, I can't stop thinking about that poor family; we killed them. And now here we are having the time of our lives." She sat up.

"I'd debate that!" Richard realized the good times were over, at least for now. "Okay, I can understand how you feel. But don't let it take over your life." He reached for his clothes. "Let me know when you can start thinking about us and not those victims. It was an accident, plan and simple."

"I'll try, but I'll tell you, it may take one hell of a long time for me to find making love a pleasurable experience!"

"Well, whatever it takes in time, just concentrate on your life, on our life, and not theirs."

"Like I said I'll try." Becky began sobbing quietly, as Richard finished dressing and went down to the street."

Wanda was standing there looking around the parking lot. She saw Richard and came over. "Honey, come home, I'm sorry I made you leave." She hugged him.

"It's all right Wanda, we'll get through this, it will make us stronger."

"Where is Becky, I want to apologize to her?"

"She stayed in her room; she wasn't feeling well after her breakfast. I think the fact that people lost their lives because of the accident, is making it hard for her to get back to normal."

"What about you? Is it affecting you?"

"Oh, yes, I'm having nightmares about the night of the accident" He generated a few tears as he took her by the arm. "Let's go home, Honey."

"I'll look after you Dear." She reached for his car keys; here, I'll drive us home."

"Thanks Dear, I won't forget this day."

CHAPTER 5

After a year of inquiries and further police investigation, the pair was charged with negligent homicide they were to be tried together. The presiding Judge was Roy Hamilton.

Sean Hardy, Prosecutor for the Crown didn't waste anytime in trivial matters. "As Captain of the vessel, did you have both hands on the wheel before during and after the impact?"

Captain Selby answered politely, "I was in the wheelhouse."

"Were you steering the vessel?"

"Yes."

"Then you must have had both hands on the wheel?"

"I suppose?"

"Would you elaborate on your statement, did you or did you not have both hands on the wheel?"

"I don't remember?"

"You're the Captain of a vessel and you don't remember? Is it a case of refusing to answer truthfully?"

"It's my right to refuse to answer, so I'm invoking that right."

Frustrated the prosecutor turned to the Judge. "No more questions for this witness."

Becky proved to be just as uncooperative, she admitted to being in the brig, but refused to divulge any information on their activities.

The prosecutor had one final line of questioning. "Miss Morris, is it not a fact that you and Captain Selby are lovers?"

"We were, several years ago."

"What about on October, 15, 2010, the date the Northern Cross sank?"

"We were working the same shift, on the same crew; we were both in the wheelhouse."

"I'll repeat the question, more clearly. Were there any discussions or actions occurring between you and Captain Selby between 11 p.m. October15, and 2 a.m. October 16th, 2009, relating to romantic discussions or activities?"

"I refuse to answer that question, on the grounds that it may incriminate me."

"You just did." He turned to the defense table, "I'm finished with this witness."

The defense attorney, Shelia Hobson stood up. "Objection, the prosecutor is speculating and drawing conclusions."

"Objection sustained, the prosecutor's last remark will be stricken from the record and the jury is instructed to disregard it in its entirety."

Hobson rose again, "Your Honor, may we approach the bench?"

"Please do." Sean Hardy and Shelia Hobson stepped forward.

"I 'm making a motion for a mistrial. The Prosecutor's remark which is an unproven speculation may have influenced the jury to the point that they cannot reach a fair verdict."

Sean Hardy countered, "Your Honor, the jury received your instructions, the witness's uncooperative manner caused the doubt, she should not benefit from her own silence."

"Be seated, I will poll the Jury." Judge Hamilton turned to address the Jury. "Ladies and Gentlemen of the Jury, I am asking you to consider the remark that the Prosecutor made, and if you feel that you cannot disregard that question later when making your deliberations and wish to be excused, let the Bailiff know. Court is adjourned for 30 minutes."

Court reconvened; none of the Jury members disqualified themselves. "Will the Prosecutor call his next witness?"

"I call Captain Selby." Selby was sworn in. " Captain Selby, while you were in command of the Northern Cross ferry, was there any discussions or actions occurring between you and your first mate, Becky Morris, between 11 p.m. of October15, and 2 a.m. of October 16th, of 2009, relating to romantic discussions or activities?"

"I refuse to answer that question, on the grounds that it may incriminate me."

"Are you and Miss Morris, conspiring to cover up evidence in connection with the sinking of the Northern Cross vessel?

"I refuse to answer that question, on the grounds that it may incriminate me."

"Your witness." The prosecutor took his seat, waiting for the defense to minimize the damage; the witness's refusal to answer questions had created.

Sheila Hobson had little wiggle room. "Captain tell the court how long you have been a captain with the Ferry Service?

"Eighteen years."

"How many years on the Inside Passage route?"

"Just over 9 years."

"How many accidents did the vessels under your command have, beside this one on October 15?"

"None, none at all?"

"Thank you Captain, no more questions."

"Redirect your Honor."

Judge Hamilton nodded.

"Captain, in those 18 years how many times was Becky Morris posted on your watch as the first mate, in your wheel house with you?"

"None."

"So the one time you and Miss Morris were on the same watch, you incurred the first accident in your 18 year career?"

"Objection, the Prosecutor's question is not relevant."

"Oh, but it is, Objection overruled, the witness will answer the question."

"Yes."

"Yes you incurred your first accident with Miss Morris in the wheelhouse with you."

"That is correct, it was foggy,"

"In your 9 years on that route was it ever foggy on any of your runs?"

"Of course, many times."

"How many?"

"I can't say."

"Take a wild guess, records show you made 55 runs, how many were in foggy weather, 10, 20, 30?= give me a number?"

"I'd estimate between 15 and 20."

"So you navigated that passage approximately 35 to 40 times without any problems?"

"Yes."

"Was it because you had more experienced First Mates on those runs?"

"No, I would not say that."

"Then what was the reason for the accident on October 15?"

"Objection."

"Sustained, that matter has already been asked in your prior questioning."

"No more questions."

Court adjourned for the day.

As they were leaving the courtroom, Becky slipped a note to Richard, it had five words. *I need to see you.*

CHAPTER 6

Richard was confused; there had been no personal contact between him and Becky for almost a year. Richard had deemed her non-contact as a sign that they were through, as far as any romantic liaisons were concerned. *Now here was this very provocative message! What did Becky want? Was it about the trial matter? Was it about them and their future?*

He went down the street to Monty's Bar and had a Rum and Coke, then he had two more, then he decided it was time to call Becky. He asked the manager/owner, "Bryan, can I make a local call from your office?"

"Sure Buddy, don't drown in the mess of paperwork lying around!" He chuckled.

Becky answered on the first ring. "Where are you? I was hoping to here from you a couple of hours ago."

"I'm in a bar drinking! In any case, what was the urgency about needing to see me?"

"I've been thinking and I have decided to plead guilty to the charges. I want to make a full disclosure of what happened that night in the wheelhouse."

"Hold on now Becky! Let's discuss this. If you cop a plea, then they will ask you to testify against me. Are you sure that's what you want?"

Becky sounded quite convincing "If it lets me sleep at night, then yes, I will do it."

"Look Becky, may I come over so we can talk this out face to face?"

"I've made up my mind Richard" She was adamant. "I just thought you should know, before I talk to our lawyer."

"Stay there, I am on my way over. I'll be there in ten minutes."

"Come if you insist, but I'm pretty certain I want to tell everything."

Richard was considering all his options as he drove down to Becky's apartment. *How can I make her realize she is harming not only herself but me as well! Do I have to kill the bitch, to keep her from blabbing? That's crazy, I have to talk her out of it, that's all, there must be a better way of shutting her up.*

Richard's palms were perspiring as he knocked loudly on her door.

Becky opened the door. "Come in Richard, I don't want the neighbors to see you?"

"We haven't been convicted yet, we are out on bail, remember?"

"Never mind that, what did you want to say?"

"I don't want you blabbing to the court about that night. How can I convince you that it is not in the best interest of either one of us to have you turning us in? Now I repeat, how can I keep you from doing that?"

Becky, smiling in an inviting somewhat embarrassed manner replied. "There are two ways."

"And what are they, tell me, what's this entire dramatization leading up to." Again, he saw an impish look on Becky's face. "What the hell, are you up to? What are the two ways?"

"Firstly, you could kill me!" She chuckled at the absurd thought of Richard choking her to death.

"I've considered that, but I've ruled it out." He thought the humor of his remark would shake her up. She waited for him to speak again. "What is the other way?"

"Guess?"

"Becky, this isn't a game show, now out with it, what have you cooked up?" Richard was becoming annoyed.

"I want you to divorce Wanda, and then marry me as soon as you're free of her."

"Are you crazy?"

"You once said you didn't really love her, that loyalty was your only reason for keeping the marriage alive."

"I may have said that one or two times but that doesn't mean I'd drop everything and divorce her."

"Those are your choices, marry me or go to prison!"

"That is the flaw in your stupid scheme; we'll be imprisoned for fifteen years or more. You'll be in prison right alongside me!"

"They don't allow co-ed prisons; we'll have to write each other." Becky grinned.

"Don't crack jokes, Becky. Are you that determined that you would sit in prison and hope to reconnect when we both got out? That is an idiotic plan! Now let's find another way!"

Becky had given Richard an ultimatum, standing up she motioned Richard to leave. "You have until tomorrow morning when court reconvenes. Otherwise, I will fire my lawyer and get a new one. Goodnight Richard, I know you'll do the right thing." She gave him a peck on the cheek and closed the door after him.

Richard now realized why Becky has been standoffish for the past months; she had been cooking up this devious plan to get him to marry her. He was caught in the twilight zone. It did not feel very comforting. He had his choice, divorce his wife and then agree to marry Becky and spend perhaps the next fifteen years in prison.

It was time to have a sincere talk with Wanda. She would know what to do. He drove home and repeated Becky's offer to her.

"Richard, this is of your own doing! I should let you wallow in your own filth darling, but here is what you can do. Let Becky tell her story, then you can deny it, it's your word against hers. I will be happy to testify on your behalf that we have a happy marriage, and that I had no knowledge of her and you having any affair, and I think the whole thing is preposterous."

"Will that work?"

"It's the best thing, unless you want me to go over there and strangle Little Miss Moffat?"

"No, we aren't strangling anyone! In the morning I will tell her you're aware of her plan, and you will stand by me no matter what."

"Now, tell me did that accident happen while you and her were making out?"

Richard was cornered. "Yes, the rumors to that effect are completely true. I'm so sorry Honey."

"You think you're sorry now, wait a couple of months and you'll know what sorry really feels like." Wanda, gave him an *I gotcha where I want you* stare.

Richard cursed the day he thought women were all darlings, exciting and everything pleasant.

CHAPTER 7

Richard had a meeting with Sheila Hobson, his attorney, informing her of Becky's intentions of pleading guilty and telling all. He didn't tell her of Becky's ultimatum to marry her or Becky's threat to plead guilty and tell all.

"I'll see what I can do, however, once she gets another lawyer then I have no more control over her. If she testifies against you then your case is very weak. You may want to cut a deal yourself and beat her to it. This is between you and me, technically I still represent her."

"See what the prosecutor can do for me or for both of us for that matter? Then tomorrow morning we can see if Becky follows through on her threat?"

Sean Hardy was cool to Sheila Hobson's suggestion, Sheila didn't tell him about Becky's threat. Sean did compromise. "I'll agree to a reduction of the charge from negligent homicide to involuntary manslaughter. Captain Selby does seven years, and has to agree to give testimony against Miss Morris, if necessary. I'll extend the same deal to Miss Morris, as well."

"I'll run it by them, and will have an answer for you tomorrow before court resumes."

Wednesday morning saw Shelia Hobson and Richard Selby meeting outside the courtroom building. She relayed the plea offer to Richard and added "Let's see what Becky thinks of the same deal."

"Here she comes now." Richard saw Becky and a stranger approaching.

Becky spoke first, "Richard can I talk to you privately, for a moment?" They walked a short distance and she asked "Well, are you taking my offer, or do I talk?"

"Sorry Becky, I can't see that working out for you or for me. Sheila Hobson has an offer from the Prosecutor to reduce the charges." He looked at her for a moment, "I will go with that before agreeing to your zany proposal. She said you can get the same deal."

"Screw you, Hobson and the Prosecutor. I've got a new lawyer, and I can make a better deal." Beck could see she her contrived plan was losing ground

Richard dismissed her, "Then there is nothing further to say! This is where we part company. I'll hang back while you go talk to Sheila." He turned and walked a few steps farther away, while Becky approached Shelia and the Stranger.

Becky addressed the pair, "Miss Hobson this is Craig Stevens, he is taking over my case."

"Yes, he has introduced himself to me. As far as your case, yes, that is your right to change attorneys and we will inform the court accordingly. Now, do you know that I have an offer of a lesser plea?"

"Richard told me he had a deal, tell Craig here what it is and we'll go from there."

Craig Stevens interjected, "Look Becky, if the plea agreement sounds interesting to the point of you agreeing then you don't need me. You can finish it up with Miss Hobson here."

"I want you here, Craig." Becky turned to Sheila, "What is the deal."

"The charge would be reduced to involuntary manslaughter and you serve seven years."

"Is Richard taking the deal?"

"He's leaning that way?"

"Then he would be testifying against me?"

"Yes, he would have to agree to that if you continue with the trial."

"That bastard, do you know I told him yesterday that I wanted to make full disclosure, but him, no, not him, he just wanted to continue covering up the wheelhouse happening Now he has trumped me, and he will be testifying against me, personally that sucks."

"He hasn't agreed to anything yet, you can both still stand your ground and let the trial continue."

Becky turned to Craig, "Do you have any suggestions?"

"I would have to see what evidence has accumulated against you, before I can venture an opinion." Craig was carful with his words.

"Nobody knows shit-all, while we were in the wheel house when the ferry ran aground in the fog. I think we might get a hung jury with so little to go on."

"Don't count on that." Craig replied "When there is loss of life, as in this case, the jury is looking for a reason to provide justice for the victims' families. You may be best advised to consider accepting a plea, especially if Captain Selby takes the deal. If he testifies against you, it blows your defense, of an unforeseeable accident, out of the water. Pardon my choice of words."

Miss Hobson motioned Richard to meet her a short distance away, "Becky's about to agree to the plea, how about you?"

"If we can end this here, and you think it is the best I can expect then I will accept."

"Craig her new attorney, had a good point, he feels the jury will lean toward getting justice for the family that died. They may be hard to convince. Your chances of a not guilt verdict seem remote, at best."

"Then go ahead finalize the plea deal."

"You are aware that you will have to make full disclosure of what happened in the wheelhouse the day of the accident?"

"If that what it takes, then yes, I will give a brief, factual, description of what happened."

Judge Hamilton, apprised of the plea agreement, convened court and asked Becky Morris to appear before him. "I understand that you have agreed to plead guilty to involuntary manslaughter?"

Becky head bowed answered in a low voice. "Yes Your Honor."

"Tell the court what happened."

"I was romantically involved with Captain Selby, instead of paying attention to the course the ferry was set on. As a result of my inattentiveness an accident happened, which may have been avoided if I had been doing my duties as First Mate. That is everything, Your Honor. I apologize to the Court for my actions."

"Very well," the Judge hesitated as he sorted through his papers. "Miss Becky Morris, I hereby sentence you to a term of seven years in a prison facility to be determined by Provincial authorities. You may resume your seat."

Captain Richard Shelby was next, and he went through the same routine of agreeing to a plea agreement and describing what transpired.

"Very well," the Judge hesitated again as he sorted through his papers once again. "Captain Richard Selby, I find your conduct in neglecting your duties as Captain abhorrent, and I hereby sentence you to a term of fifteen years in a prison facility to be determined by Provincial authorities. You Sir, may take your seat."

Shelia Hobson rose. "Pardon me Your Honor; my client had a plea agreement, for a prison term of seven years."

"Not with me he didn't! His plea agreement was not conditional on his agreeing only if I concurred, you overlooked that point. It is my right to vary the sentence, and my sentence of fifteen years stands. Court is adjourned."

Richard Selby was shocked as he returned to the defense table. 'What happened Miss. Hobson?"

"The judge was correct in law, In the hurriedness of making up the papers I forgot to include the conditional clause."

"This is ridiculous, Becky gets seven years, I get fifteen?"

"I'm sorry, we can't change it." She offered a suggestion. "All we can do is press for an early parole; the board may take the change into account when we present the application to them."

"When will that happen?"

"After you serve 1/3 of your sentence."

"5 years?"

"Yes."

Captain Selby slumped in his chair, "God what a way to finish my career, I'm 52 in fifteen years I'll be 67, I'm done!" He was led away by the court custodian to a cell for transfer to the prison yet to be determined. Becky had been likewise led away after she made her declaration and sentencing.

CHAPTER 8

3 years later

Becky having served one third of her sentence was granted parole after serving 28 months. She managed to gain employment with a tourist company that offered cruises up and down the inside passage. She arranged to visit Richard at the prison farm twenty miles east of Vancouver, the visitation rules were rather relaxed, as none of the offenders were at risk of being repeat offenders. In fact, it was not uncommon for couples to meet in the woods adjoining the prison buildings for some 'afternoon delight.'

Becky waited at a picnic area while the clandestine arrangements were being made to allow Richard to meet her. After about twenty minutes, Richard strolled down a pathway and came over to her. He smiled and greeted her without any animosity, "How are you doing Becky? God it's good to see you!"

"I'm fine Richard; I'm at peace with myself. I'll never forget the accident and those poor people that died, but that was yesterday and it's time to stop looking in the rear view mirror and time to look ahead. Now, Richard, you, you look fit and trim, is there anything that I can bring you the next time I come?"

"How about apple pie, my wife used to bring me the tastiest pie you can imagine."

"Used to, doesn't she come anymore?"

"She filed for divorce a year after I got sent up here."

"Oh, I'm sorry to hear that, Richard."

"Well, that too is in the past, like you said we have to look to the future!"

"And what do you see in your future?"

"I'm eligible for parole in another year and a half."

"What will you do?"

"I'm eligible for a pension. I may travel to whatever extent my parole agreement allows. Other than that who knows what lies in my future or yours for that matter."

They gazed in each other's eyes, there was no mistaking the message in both their fixed stares. They were both somewhere else, the road back to the world of unbridled love was blocked, and they both accepted it.

"Okay then Richard, I have to go now," She smiled ever so faintly, "Apple pie next Wednesday."

"I'll be here waiting, bring some whipped cream as well." Richard stood up to walk back to join a guard waiting a discreet 100 yards away...

"Anything, for a friend," Becky turned and slowly made her way back to her car...

They had stretched the rubber band of love so far that it could not regain its elasticity.

The End

POETIC JUSTICE

CHAPTER 1

The courtroom was almost deserted. A public defender, Doug Straight, hung around in one area, on the off chance he would be called upon to appear for someone.

The reporter's area was to say the least, sparsely attended. It consisted of one pimple faced male kid that looked so young you would think he hadn't yet begun to shave. The other reporter sitting on the opposite end of the reporters' section, was a sixty some thing, grandmother type, Grace Newby, who was working as a freelance reporter for the Chicago Tribune newspaper. She had recently been widowed and decided she had a story or two to tell, before her clock stopped ticking.

The assistant D.A. walked in with an armful of mostly petty, annoying case files. He had been up all night, organizing the police reports and other pertinent information on each of the fourteen cases that had been dumped on his desk a scant forty-eight hours earlier.

The bedraggled defendants began arriving for their arraignments, some had lawyers, and some looked to the public defender fill-in. Others, yet, were so confident they came in alone, expecting to represent themselves. Perhaps, they had watched too many Perry Mason TV shows when they were young, or alternatively they were just plain stupid for thinking they could adequately represent themselves!

Judge Lawrence Greenson hadn't seen a scene like this in years. He was accustomed to presiding over serious cases, such as murders, rapes, armed robberies and embezzlement cases. He had volunteered to fill in for a few days while some vacancies in the lower courts were being filled.

He looked at his agenda, four speeding, tickets, three red light traffic infractions, one disturbing the peace, four vandalism cases, one minor assault, and one for soliciting for the purpose of prostitution and keeping a common bawdyhouse.

These should keep me busy until lunchtime, he guessed. Then he looked again at the last case, the name of the defendant, Jane Morningstar, leaped off the page! He recognized the name immediately. After all how common was the name Morningstar? He looked around the small courtroom. There she was, prettier than ever. She wasn't that different from when she had worked on his re-election case four years earlier. They had been close then, too close, after two brief secret sexual encounters they agreed to break off their relationship. He never forgot her! Everything was coming back as he relived those two exciting sensual liaisons with Jane. Could they reestablish their relationship? Did he want to? Every nerve in his body shivered at the possibility of reigniting the love flame. Does the fact she was up on prostitution related charges change his feelings for her? Not one bit, she was an angel in his eyes. She would be his Angel!

I'm a judge, for god's sake why am I thinking like this? Do your job Larry, and stop daydreaming."

The bailiff, "This Court is now in session "Judge Greenson, snapped out of his trance, banging with his gavel he announced. " Send in the first case."

There was no need to send in anyone, they were all there. The bailiff called the first case, "Jimmy Jackson"

Jim was a know-it-all, 'I'll defend myself' kind of person; he advanced in front of the judge.

The bailiff announced. The charge is speeding."

The Judge looked down and in a stern voice barked, "How do you plead?"

"No,not,not- guil-guil-guilty" Jimmy Jackson had suddenly contracted a case of the stutters.

The Judge sensing an opportunity to scare the kid senseless demanded "What did you say son?"

The startled youngster, lost his resolve, this was no place to test his knowledge of the law, "Guilty as charged, your Honor." He replied in a clear voice, his stuttering was cured and his trial was over.

"Pay the fine of $200 , at the cashier's window in the hall, on your way out son, and I don't want to see you back in here anytime soon! Do you understand me?"

"Yes, Your Honor, thank you Your Honor."

The Judge took a smile break, then turned serious once again, "Next ca-cas-case." *God I'm doing it now,* he thought

"Don Stewart, the charge is disturbing the peace, and Violation of a court order." Don advanced in front with his fancy suited lawyer leading the way.

"How do you plead?"

The silk suit answered, "My client pleads not guilty, Your Honor."

"So, entered, how does the crown feel about bail?"

"The defendant, was stalking his former girlfriend. There was a restraining order out against him."

His lawyer decided to interject, "My client won't be causing any more problems" he assured the court.

Judge Greenson saw the smirk on the defendant's face. "You can count on that Counselor, this is Friday, bail is denied until Monday morning, let the young fellow calm down and realize the seriousness of his actions."

"Your Honor, my client has strong ties to the community, he does volunteer work on the weekends."

"Good, he can volunteer down at the lockup. Don't keep them waiting." Judge Greenson realized how much he had enjoyed adjudicating small cases.

He pounded his gavel. "Next case."

"Jane Morningstar" the bailiff added, "Charged with one count of keeping a common bawdyhouse".

Jane Morningstar proceeded forward; the D.A. motioned the public defender to join her. The defendant had recognized the Judge. She smiled ever so faintly."

"How does the defendant plead?"

Looking embarrassed she replied "Not guilty, Your Honor."

"Does the Prosecutor have any objection to bail."

"The bail is set at five thousand dollars."

The lawyer led Jane Morningstar away, he whispered some message in her ear, presumably about arranging the bail money, as a custodian led her away. She glanced back and saw Judge Greeson following her with his eyes. She knew from the look in his eyes she would be hearing from him very soon.

CHAPTER 2

Judge Greenson, was hard pressed to explain to himself his almost addict-like attitude toward Jane Morningstar. Was it just a case of him working too hard, under too much stress, and this was a way for his mind and body to create a diversion that would relax him?

Maybe it was just old- fashioned lust, felt by an aging professional, whose career was in its last few years. Whatever it was, he had better get control of his senses and stay out of this case. Even as he thought that, he was marking the Morningstar case down in his calendar as his case. He had seniority and, by God, if he wanted the Morningstar case he could have it!

His mind kept travelling back four years to those two blind blowing encounters he and Jane had shared. Was his reason for wanting to stay on the case to help and old friend or was the reason his desire to worm his way back into her life?

After all he was a lonely man, his wife, Meg, had passed away two years earlier after a lengthy illness. Perhaps it was time for him to stop looking in the rear view mirror and look to the road ahead. Jane Morningstar could be in his future, at least, he hoped she might be. It was good to feel robust and energetic with something to look forward to, after two, mindless work filled, years.

Jane, arranged her bail with the help of, Doug Straight, the public defender. She liked his youthful exuberance and non-judgmental attitude. Perhaps she would get better service from an experienced trial attorney; however, she thought Doug would go the extra distance in preparing her case. She told him so " Mr. Straight, I want you to defend me in this case."

"Well, I appreciate your confidence, ma'am , and I want the case, however I must admit to you I am rather inexperienced , I don't want to put you at risk!"

"Doesn't your firm have a criminal law specialist?"

"I work for my dad's law office and we specialize in real estate contracts and business litigation. I'm the only one in the office that has any interest in criminal law."

"You'll do just fine, I want you on the case." Jane had a good feeling about Straight.

"Yes, Ma'am, I'll confer with the Prosecutor and see if we can get the charges against you reduced to simple soliciting, would you agree to that and a suspended sentence?"

"Yes, I'd agree, it would be the logical thing to do. See if it can happen."

Later that evening Jane received a telephone call.

"This is Larry Greenson, Jane, how are you?"

"I've been better; I apologize for ending up in your courtroom today. I'll bet that was a shocker for you, wasn't it?" Her voice still exuded that honey-tone that Larry remembered so well.

"Let's say a mild surprise. Now before we talk any further, Jane, I want you to know that this call is off the record. I'm phoning as a friend, a friend wishing to help you."

"I understand that, and I appreciate any advice you can throw my way, I got the young kid to defend me, he may need a few pointers."

"Tell him to plead the charge down to a lesser charge, say solicitation."

"He has already suggested that!"

"Then I will casually encourage the prosecutor to cooperate, if he, mind you, if he brings it up. I can't take the initiative on this and approach him. I'm going to arrange to be the presiding judge."

"I feel better already. Now, let's talk about old times. By the way how is your family?"

"My wife passed two years ago. The kids are fine all grown up and married. I have four grand children. Now, how about you, Jane?'

"Sorry to hear about your wife! Me? I was divorced eight months ago, that is what began this ill advised erotic dating service that I set up. I guess I should have sought proper legal advice before setting up such a risky undertaking."

"Is it still operating?"

"No, I pulled all the advertising this morning; cancelled the phone lines; and laid off all the escorts. We are out of business."

"Make sure your lawyer, passes all that on to the prosecutor."

"I'll do that, and thanks for calling Larry. I guess I'll see you in court soon."

"I'd rather it was in a fine dining establishment. I know a place in the north side of the city. I'd like to invite you to join me for a dinner and dance there. "

"Is that not taking a chance? You being the Judge and all?"

"I'll wear my Dick Tracy disguise." Larry laughed. "Come on say yes, how about Tuesday night? Please."

Jane relented, "If you're sure it wouldn't complicate your life, Larry."

"Being lonely is the complication, Jane, I really need you!" Greenson had made his feelings known. "

"I agree then," Jane, cooed , I'll expect you to pick me up at my home, at say 6.30, Apartment 303 ,4555 Brighton Ave.,"

"Thanks a bunch, Jane, I'm looking forward to Tuesday."

"Goodnight Larry."

CHAPTER 3

On Monday morning, Doug Straight contacted Rod Green, the assistant prosecutor and discussed a plea agreement with him relating to Jane Morningstar's charges. He also related the information about Jane having closed the escort agency venture." So what do you think? Can your office reassess the charges and lower them down a couple of notches."

"I'll check with my superior, I think your proposal will get some favorable consideration I'll recommend it. I see by my file here that she started this service only two weeks ago. I guess the vice squad jumped all over her, literally speaking of course. It barely got started, so I think your request will be accepted."

"Thanks Rod, I owe you one."

"No problem, buddy. Just remember that when we meet again." Rod chuckled.

By 3.30 p.m., Rod received a call. "It's not a deal Rod. The prosecutor, Don Johnston, won't relent on this one. In fact, he's taking charge of the case. I don't know what his motivation is, perhaps political, in any event start preparing her case. The case is slated for August 19, three months from now. We drew Judge Greenson, and we better be well prepared, he's tough on these sorts of charges."

Straight was disappointed, he thought he had served his client well; however, the D.A.'s office was unsatisfied, the vice squad must have objected to their work being undervalued. He would do his best to get Jane Morningstar an acquittal on the overblown charges. He Called Jane and advised her of the decision.

She sounded disappointed, "Maybe the judge will see the case in a different light, I will elect to be tried by a Judge alone, not by a

Jury. I have another suggestion, start volunteering for some charity or other community organization. We have to build up your reputation as a willing community supporter." He looked at her sternly, "Juries can sometime have a sympathetic member or two that can get you an acquittal.".

"I trust in the law, let the judge handle it." Morningstar was firm on that point.

"I don't agree, however, If those are you instructions, I will proceed accordingly." Straight was confused, *what does she know that I don't know?* Then he remembered the familiar glances she had exchanged with Judge Greenson, on the day of her arraignment. Perhaps it would be prudent not to delve into their personal history. *If there was sympathy in the judge's heart for his client, why should he not play up that sympathy for the benefit of his client?*

Larry Greenson, arrived a fifteen minutes early at Jane's apartment. Parking his BMW in the visitor's stall, he made his way to the lobby and took the elevator to the third floor. Apartment 303 was directly across from the elevator. He rang the bell, no answer, he decided he might have caught her at an inopportune time. He strolled down to the end of the hall. There was a beverage-dispensing machine there. He deposited $1.25 and selected a bottle of spring water. Unscrewing the top, he took a swig of its' contents and replaced the lid. He heard a door close back up the hall, he turned and saw a young, tall, blonde man standing in front of the elevator. At the same time, he saw the door of #303 close softly.

A fleeting thought flashed through Greenson's mind. *Why would she have company just before an expected visit? Oh, stop being a jealous bastard. She must have had a good reason to have someone call on her.* He lingered at the drink machine for another five minutes then went back and rang her doorbell.

"Come in Larry. I'm glad to see you, I'll be another ten minutes or so, you don't mind do you?"

"Of Couse not, there are no set times at this country place."

"You're a dear," she give him a peck on the cheek, "Have a seat in the living room, the remote is on the coffee table If you want to watch television. Would you care for a drink?"

"No, I have a bottle of water here. I'm fine." He gazed at her swaying hips as she left the room.

He glanced around to see if anything in the room pointed to the identity of Jane's visitor. The ashtray was clean, the magazine stand was well arranged, the faint smell of man's shaving lotion, though pleasant, did not prove anything. He walked over to a paper strewn , smaller, desk, probably the center of operations for the now defunct 'escort agency'. The Day-Timer on the desk was open to today's date. He glanced at it, and was flabbergasted, it had a number of appointments, ,actually a total of five. The first was Bell, 10 that morning, then Cuddles at 11, Mort at 1 and so on , and the last appointment was Chuck at 5.30. Was that Chuck that he saw leaving the apartment?

Greenson was taken aback. *She's conducting business as usual he assumed, what is she doing, acting as though she is a little innocent Miss. Angel, when it appears she is a full time call girl.* He quickly stepped away from the desk and sat in the Lazy-boy rocker, grabbed a magazine and tilted back the chair.

"I'm ready, honey." Jane cooed as she reappeared, dressed in a stunning, low cut black lacy-topped evening dress, with a black pearl necklace gracing the open area of her upper chest.

"Wow!" was all Larry could say as he helped her put on a summer wrap before leaving the apartment. As they took the elevator down Larry began asking gentle probing questions. "How are you going to manage, Jane, you have no income now?"

"Oh, I have a few dollars, and I'll manage, maybe I can get some work on the campaign teams for the fall elections. Perhaps you can recommend me, you said I did a good job on yours"

Larry blushed at the double meaning of her statement. "I was more than satisfied, Jane, you know that." He too, could speak in double meaning phrases.

"Who are we kidding?" She snuggled up against him as they approached the car. "We're one of a kind, alone and needing someone."

"I have to agree with you there, Jane. Everyone needs someone."
The old familiarity was there once again. There were no obstacles to
a mutually enjoyable evening. They both knew it.

Did they both sincerely want that? Greenson certainly did! Was
Jane playing him for the favors she might get in the courtroom in
a couple of months. He decided to enjoy the moment, why worry
about tomorrow, or next week or the following months? He aimed
the BMW northward and accelerated up road to happiness. Within
twenty minutes, he was parking in the underground parkade of the
Le Passage.

Le Passage, a dance club, with an upscale restaurant, featured a
dance floor and live bands amidst a dark but elegant setting. The
nightclub's 1930s inspired interior featured art deco light fixtures
and wood beam ceilings. The restaurant offered a gourmet menu, including such dishes as sautéed scallops, veal nuggets and pan-roasted
chicken.

Larry Greenson and Jane Morningstar strolled up to the maître
de. "Good evening folks, have you a reservation?

Greenson replied. "Yes we do, it's Larry Grayson," he thought it
prudent to use his mother's maiden name.

"Ah yes, here we are. Follow me please. I have a quiet corner table
for as you requested." He led them to a dimly lit semi partition area.
"Will this do?" He motioned them to have a seat.

Greenson nodded his approval, "Excellent, thank you." He assisted Jane with her chair.

"Thanks Larry, this is really nice! I haven't been here before."

"We came here occasionally." Greenson said, referring to his late
wife.

CHAPTER 4

The evening was everything Larry had imagined and more. They had cocktails, " a toast to a beautiful lady" Larry raised his glass.

In jest, Jane looked over her left shoulder as though looking for the subject of the toast. She turned back to Larry with a grin on her face, "Oh, you mean me!" She winked as they clicked glasses.

The server brought menus and they selected their meal, Jane ordered the scallops and Larry settled for the pan roasted chicken. While they waited for their meal, the dance, the band struck up a dance tune , Marty Robin's 'White Sport Coat.' It was one of Larry's favorite, "Shall we dance." He suggested rising to his feet.

"By all means." Jane joined him and they walked out on the floor. Several other couples had preceded them. " This is lovely," she cooed, as they glided down the dance floor. "I haven't danced like this for some time."

"Me neither."

"Thanks for asking me out."

"You know you were always my favorite lady!"

"Then this is where we should be, let's enjoy the evening." The dance ended and they returned to their table, to enjoy the meal that was promptly served. After their meal, they continued dancing for two hours. They left the club with a glow usually associated with young couples in love

Larry discounted his earlier thoughts of Jane using her felinity to influence him. He basked in the sweet talk and attention she was heaping on him. "Where were you twenty years ago when I needed you?" She joked.

Let me see now, I had graduated from law school and served my two-year practicum with Nobel, Chard, and Dugan, and a further ten years of practice with them I never made partner. So I was a near penniless Jr. Lawyer, not a very attractive prize I must say!"

'When did you meet your wife?"

"Ah yes , she was one of the secretaries in the steno pool at that office. She was the only good thing that happened, from working there. We married, several years later when I got a partnership position with another firm. Those early married years were happy years, some of my best."

"Lovely memories, Larry, hold onto them; even better add to them. Now let's have one more dance before we go back to my place." They danced to the instrumental version of "Save the Last Dance for Me." Larry was delighted with the evening, and even happier that it promised to continue , well into the night, back at Jane's apartment.

The drive back to City Center was filled with good-natured banter back and forth between them as they relaxed knowing they were heading for cloud nine territory.

🕮

"You'll find some condoms in the top drawer of the nightstand on your side there." Jane directed in an almost work supervisor tone.

They had been in bed only a few minutes, so the remark caught Larry by surprise, " I'm not ready for that yet, sweetie," he cautioned.

In the darkness, he could not see the red blush that covered Jane's face, when she realized she had used words and tones that she normally applied to her escort clients. 'Sorry dear, of course, just let me know when you're ready. She snuggled up against him, barring her breasts near his upper body so he could luxuriate in his fantasies. She had forgotten how soothing it felt to be made love to by a partner that truly felt the closeness and wanted her as well as her favors.

Even though Larry was sixty, he exhibited the energy of a much younger man, as the excitement of a younger woman's body spread throughout his body. Jane came out of her detached state and joined in the pleasure of the minutes as they give each other everything they had. It was as though the four years they had been apart had only been a matter of days, they moved in rhythm to each other's thrusts and totally lost themselves in their final effort to reaching a fully satisfying simultaneous climax.

Larry was 'zoned out 'He didn't believe that such ecstasy would ever be his to again enjoy . "Janey, Honey , I can't describe that as being anything other than out of this world."

"I know Larry, I felt the same way." She kissed him again, "Do you want to do dance some more?"

"I would if I could, Sweetie, but I have to admit I have limitations."

"Not in my estimation!"

"Thanks for the compliment, but I'm afraid I'll have to take a rain check , how about Thursday?"

"Sure, come over at seven, I'll have dinner ready here, I know you liked roast beef."

"I still do, that will be super." They got up and showered, had a nightcap in the living room, and then Larry prepared to leave. He noticed Jane's answering machine flashing as he went past her desk. He wondered what the messages were about. Jane had not bothered to check them on their arrival back from the restaurant.

After Jane closed the door, Larry lingered to listen. He heard Jane walk across the laminate floor and activate the answering machine. "Jane, this is Doc, I'll be there at ten for my regular visit." The second message was "This is Big Daddy 13, I'll phone you in the morning, for an appointment at say 3 tomorrow afternoon. Larry had heard enough, his glow began subsiding, Jane, his hope for the future, had a few skeletons , or rather a few live ones, in her closet. He would have to think twice about this; then he decided right there. *After a night like that, what was there to think about? He was hooked , damn the legalities ,this was his last chance at happiness and by God, he was going to take it.*

CHAPTER 5

Don Johnston, the prosecutor, had occasion to join Judge Greenson for coffee. Unknown to him, of course, Judge Greenson and Morningstar the accused, had been meeting twice a week for some two months now, everything was cozier that cozy.

"Judge Greenson, the Morningstar case comes up next Tuesday, they have elected to a trial by Judge. Are you still prepared to remain on the case?"

"This is a chicken-shit case, Don," he paused, "Compared to my last three years' assignments, it will be refreshing to test my memory of case law in these simpler cases."

"This trial will be fairly high profile, I have had an enquiry, from a reporter by the name of Grace Newby, of the Tribune. She knows Jane Morningstar worked on your reelection four years ago."

"Yes, she did a fine job, so did another fifty people, it has no bearing on me, my job, or the outcome of her case. " He hoped he was right.

"Very well then, I just want you to be apprised of all the facts that cross my desk., and could cause a problem for you."

"I appreciate your cooperation, Don, sure, let me know if there are any other concerns, I'll be happy to deal with them."

Judge Greenson, began delving into case law, to see what past cases he could use to support a favorable verdict for Jane. He realized he was putting the proverbial ox before the cart, however ,if he could indirectly guide Doug Straight to some pertinent case law, it might help curb Don Johnston's zealousness, it might soften him up to accept a lessor plea. He sat down in front of his computer and made a few points.

1.Get some witnesses that patronized the Escort agency to testify that other than an evening 'out 'or a conversation 'in', there wasn't anything of a sexual nature during the sessions, and testify that in their visits with Mrs. Morningstar, the topic of sexual services never came up.

2. Go over the definition of Brothel or Common Bawdy house , and show that the defendant's apartment did not, in any way, compare to a 'sex shop', such as a massage parlor, saunas, a bar, or a strip bar.

3. Try and get a deal, where she pleads guilty, have her make as an act of contrition, a donation to a charity that supports sex-trade workers in their efforts to reform and quit the business.

4. Show there was no evidence that anyone was victimized, such as under age escorts or under aged clients.

5. Have the defendant make an apology to the court

6. Then ask for an absolute discharge.

Judge Greenson , printed out the memo and mailed it to ,Doug Straight's residence, in a unmarked envelope , from a mailbox from an adjoining town.

That Tuesday evening , was Greenson's date with Jane, " Hi honey, what sort of a day did you have?" He asked in normal opening conversation like tone, as her handed her a bottle of wine.

"What do you mean?" Jane was getting rosy cheeks. Then she recovered, and smiled, taking the wine from his hand and putting it on the kitchen counter. "Oh, just a boring series of nondescript things, I can't keep my mind on anything with the trial coming up next Monday."

"I have to suggest that we can't meet or have any contact, during the period between the trial start, and say a month after the verdict, and/ or sentencing hearing."

"I understand, Jane cuddled up against him. I'll miss our little

Tuesday rendezvous, Larry. I've grown very fond of you." She helped him off with his jacket. "Would you pour us some wine, while I serve out our dinner?"

"Sure, Honey. Have you heard from your lawyer yet?"

"I got a call from him today. He said he has a few suggestions, to make about to help my case. He seems to be very adept, and confident we can get the prosecutor to cooperate and agree to something very minor. "

"Let's hope he can!" Larry smiled, "I hear you have a sympathetic judge?"

"That would help, that would help a lot. " Jane set down two servings of Roast beef and sat down." Here's to a fair and just verdict!" She raised her glass.

"Yes, dear, it will be a breeze." Larry, wondered if perhaps he was overstating Jane's chances of beating the charges. After all Don Johnston was no slouch, and he was hoping to make ' political hay' in this case. "Let's talk about us, and our future after this is all behind us." He suggested.

"You're the Judge, sweetheart, anything you want goes." She smiled, " now let's eat up, we have a fun filled evening ahead of us."

Grace Newby, was also in a career-building mode. When she was not contacted by Don Johnston's office, she began her own 'little investigation' into the comings and goings of Judge Greenson, and the accused, Jane Morningstar. It did not take long for her to realize that the visits by Judge Greenson to Jane's apartment building, on a regular basis had undertones of impropriety. She further noted the lateness of the night that Greenson usually exited the building and left for home.

In addition, she noted the hourly visitors throughout the day and night on most days when Jane was home. In addition, she further noticed the decline in visitor activity on Tuesday evenings when Judge Greenson was visiting. *Two+two makes four, or is it 10?* She thought to herself.

She contacted her Editor at the Tribune offices and apprised him of her findings. "What should I do?"

"Nothing, let the case continue and we will have our criminal lawyer advisor monitor the case and then see if he recommends us to blow the whistle on Judge Greenson."

"Isn't that almost entrapment?"

"He's doing it to himself! You didn't encourage them to begin seeing each other, did you?"

"No, of course not."

"Then we are in the clear; even though this is Chicago, this could be the biggest story of the month, stay on it, and Grace keep a low profile. You aren't Angela Lansbury you know.'"

"Not yet, Chief." Grace grinned and made a Hollywood bow , turning to exit his office.

CHAPTER 6

The trial

It was a rainy Chicago morning as Courtroom 103, was called to order. Judge Greenson called for the charges to be read, asked both parties if they were ready to proceed. Being informed they were, he asked the Prosecutor to begin.

Don Johnston, give a brief opening statement." Your Honor, we will prove that the defendant set up an Escort Agency, whose sole purpose was to provide sexual favors to clients. That she hired women to work for her agency, arranged so called 'dates' for them and lived off the avails of prostitution." Thank you your Honor.

Doug Straight, rose to give a brief statement, "Your Honor, the only case here is the over zealousness of the Chicago Police department and the Prosecutor's office. We can show that this is nothing more than a failed business venture, which my client formed with the sole undertaking to earn some income as an advisor to troubled people. Both men and women. We ask that the case be dismissed as groundless, and without substance."

Judge Greenson saw that Doug Straight, was giving him an opportunity to be seen as a tough in command Judge. "That, young fellow, will never be the case in my Courtroom!" he barked.

Doug Straight, acting indignant, slapped his file down on the desk in front of him. "Yes, Your Honor, "he snapped.

"Don't use that tone in my Court, Sir!" Another point seemingly scored by the Judge.

"I apologize to Your Honor." The defense attorney took his seat; a slight smile crossed his lips.

Don Johnston, began his case. "We call Detective Steve Morgan to the stand." He was sworn in.

"You were the arresting Officer in this case, were you not?"

"Yes, Sir."

"I this the report you filed?" He handed the Detective the report.

"Yes."

"Would you state the circumstances that led up to your laying charges against the defendant."

Detective Morgan, began, " On July 6th of this year, I placed a call to a telephone number which appeared in the Tribune, under the classified column "Personals'."

"What did the ad say?"

"I have it here; it says, Attractive women available to assist men in overcoming their inhibitions. Satisfaction guaranteed. Call 708-739-7399."

"If you convert the numbers 739 to letters on the phone what do you get?"

"SEX"

"So the seven digit number reads 'sex-sexy', is that not rather suggestive?"

"Objection, that is sheer speculation, other letters could apply!"

"Objection sustained. The witness is appearing to state the facts, not his interpretations ." Judge Greenson, replied. " Ask another question."

Don Johnston continued," Tell us what transpired when you called the number 739-7399?"

"A female answered with the salutation '739-7399, how may we help you?' I said was calling in response to the advertisement, and I wished to have an appointment to see if I could get help. She asked what my problem was, so she could set me up with the right person on her staff. I said I was nervous around women and needed some help in overcoming a personal problem. She asked me my age, I told her 45 and she suggested I meet with her as she was of a similar age.

I got an appointment for 3 p.m. that afternoon and I met with the defendant., at her apartment # 303."

"What happened then?"

"I asked her what she charged."

"She stated and hour would cost $ 150, in advance. I held the money out to her, and asked if that included sex."

"What did she reply?"

"She didn't respond right away; however she nodded and after a few seconds answered, "I think we can help you out." At that point, she motioned me to have a seat on her sofa.

"Did you take that to mean that sex would be involved?"

"Yes, it was clear, I wasn't there to walk her dog." The few specta-tors in the courtroom began laughing.

"Order in the Courtroom." Greenson pounded with his gavel. He turned to the witness, " Just the facts Detective."

"Yes. Your Honor."

"Then what did you do?"

"I identified myself and placed the defendant under arrest."

"Your witness?"

The defense picked up on one point, " Did she actually take the money from you?"

"No, I arrested her.'

"Then there was no actual payment, just an offer of payment?"

"Yes I offered her the money."

"Did she have a bedroom?"

"Why did she ask you to have a seat on the sofa in the living room, and not ask you into the bedroom. Sex usually occurs in bed-rooms doesn't it?"

"I can't speculate on her reason."

"Did she remove any of your clothing, or her own clothing?"

"No, we remained fully clothed."

"Well, let me suggest to you, that she asked you to stay in the liv-ing room because she wanted to discuss your so called problem with you in a relaxing home like environment. Is that possible?"

"Like I said I can't say, I don't know."

"Thank you Detective, you clarified the situation for the court, payment did not change hands clothing was not removed and no form of sexual conduct or contact occurred. No more questions."

The Prosecutor had another witness." I call Mrs. Beatrice Holly to the stand."

"You live in an apartment unit across from the defendant Mrs. Morningstar?"

"Yes, I'm number 302."

"Have you noticed increased visitors to her apartment during the two weeks prior to August 6th of this year?"

"Yes, Mrs. Morningstar had almost hourly visitors. Before that she had virtually none."

"Do you know why she had suddenly attracted visitors?"

"No, I have no idea, only rumors."

"Objection, we are not interested in rumors!"

Judge Greenson agreed, "Objection sustained."

"Withdrawn."

"No more questions."

Doug Straight had only one question. "Did you hear any sounds from the apartment # 303?"

"No, never."

"Were any of Mrs. Morningstar's visitors, rowdy, or appear to be drunken, or otherwise disruptive?"

"Nothing I can recall."

"No more questions."

Judge Greenson decided it was lunchtime, " This court is adjourned until two o'clock."

"Don Johnston, saw his case was not going to be sustainable. He looked over at Doug Straight and raised his eyebrows as if saying, *do you want to talk?*

Doug, smiled and nodded, he motioned with his thumb towards Jane Morningstar, leaning over to whisper in her ear. "Jane, the Prosecutor wants to talk, do I have your authorization to negotiate a plea?"

"If it ends this embarrassment then, yes, get me out of here."

""Go to lunch, I'll meet you in the cafeteria in about fifteen minutes. Order me a BLT toasted and an iced tea. We'll celebrate."

"Doug, sit down, Don Johnston cleared a few files off a chair. These petty cases are driving me batty."

"What is your proposal? Mrs. Morningstar wants an end to this."

"Plead to immoral conduct, and serve 300 hours of community service."

"And she gets an absolute discharge?"

"I'll recommend it to Judge Greenson."

"I'll confirm this with Mrs. Morningstar, I think we have a deal."

❧

"Mrs. Morningstar, we have an offer", he detailed the offer to her. "What do you say?"

"Yes, but will the Judge accept the plea?"

"They do in 95% of these cases, they have more serious cases than this."

"I accept the deal. What's next?"

"We go back into court, the Judge will be notified before hand, and he will make it final."

"And that's it?"

"Except for some paper work. I have some advice for you Mrs. Morningstar."

"What's that?"

" Consider yourself fortunate, if you are charged again, you will be facing jail time."

"But I'm innocent!"

"Not guilty, is not innocent! That is all I have to say. Other than watch out for that reporter woman, I saw her talking to the prosecutor as I left his office."

"What are you referring to?"

"Tuesday night."

Jane went silent, she was jeopardizing Larry's status as a judge.

Judge Greenson, was pleased with the plea arrangement. " Will the defendant rise and come forward?" Jane Morningstar stood before him." I understand, you plead guilty to a charge of immoral conduct."

"Yes, Your Honor, I apologize to the court for my behavior."

"I dismiss the prior charges against you, and I accept your plea of guilty, and sentence you to do 300 hours of community service. I also place you on probation for one year. Do you understand the sentence?"

"Yes, Your Honor."

"Report to the clerk of the court. This court is adjourned."

CHAPTER 7

Don Johnston was not surprised, at Grace Newby's , information about Judge Larry Greenson's seemingly improper conduct. He had been around men and women throughout his career and had witnessed uncommon liaisons before. In fact, he himself was not completely lily-white, he thought back to his liaison with a woman professor in law school. He understood, however , he had to act on this information. He knew the Tribune, would demand answers to their questions and he wished to avoid all publicity for himself and for Judge Greenson.

That night he called the Judge at his home. " Larry, we have a problem brewing."

"Can you spell it out?"

"Your suspected affair with Jane Morningstar. The tribune is ready to go public."

"Let them, I'll sue them?"

"You're not thinking straight, Larry."

"What happened to the presumption of innocence?"

"That doesn't matter here, the public's perception is what counts. You've had a fine career, don't tarnish it by fighting this."

"What are you suggesting?"

"Resign quietly, claim some health issue, and I'll convince the tribune not to sensationalize it."

"I have to talk to Jane. Can I call you back?"

"Sure, I'll be home all evening?"

Greenson , decided to call Jane from a payphone, a mile from his home, he dialed Jane's number, 'sex –sexy' he grinned as he heard the phone ringing.

"Hello," a man's voice answered.

"Larry was surprised, Is this 379-3799 ?"

"Yes, who's calling?"

"Is Mrs. Morningstar there?"

"No, she's down in the police car. This is Detective Morgan, of the Chicago Police, Vice squad. Now sir, I'm asking you one more time to identify yourself.

Judge Greenson hung up. He could clearly see his future, it did not look promising. He called Don Johnston.

The End.

LOVE IN THE
FIRST DEGREE

CHAPTER 1

Warden Tom Ames was a man of few words. "You're fired, Miss Bristol "was his brief communication to the uncompromising woman seated across the desk.

There was no need to explain the details. A prison review board had examined the evidence. The thirty -three old, blonde-haired, Jen Bristol, who had been employed as a nurse for three years at the facility, had been caught sneaking food to an inmate, Ernest Hyman.

Ernest Hyman had spent eighteen of his past thirty-one years in one prison after another. First, it was robbery, then armed robbery, and finally confinement, rape, and murder, involving a fourteen-year-old girl, his cousin.

He was deemed incorrigible from the assessments and reports that were on top of his four-inch thick file. "His mother should have drowned him the instant she bore him!" was the speculation amongst the assessment staff that knew him. Ernest, was by far the most notorious and violent inmate in the prison's sixty year history.

The first contact between the Ernest and Jen, was destined to be the start of a lusty love relationship. It began near the end of her second year. Ernest, as he liked to be addressed, was wheeled into the infirmary during the dinner hour. Four inmates, who had a score to settle with him, had set upon him, and settle that score they did! He was bleeding profusely from every orifice in his body; his eyes were swollen shut from the punches and kicks he had sustained. Using four words 'he was a mess'.

Jen Bristol was the attending medic, and she did what her training and experience allowed, while she waited the arrival of the on call doctor to attend to the stitching and diagnosis of Ernest's internal injuries. The first words Jen uttered, when she first saw Ernest, were "Oh my God, you poor man."

Ernest, who was slipping in an out of consciousness, heard her. "It could be worse Honey!" If that wasn't the understatement of the week, then it was mighty close.

"Save your strength, cowboy," she replied, "here let me apply some compression bandages to soak up some of this mess." She compassionately went to work, and by the time Doctor Railings arrived, Ernest was almost presentable, if you can describe raw hamburger as presentable. For the next forty five minutes the good doctor, stitched, examined, and took blood tests. Then he ordered some x-rays for the following morning. The prison guards were to escort Ernest down to the Veteran's Hospital, in an ambulance, at 10 o'clock. "Give him two of these pain killers every four hours." The Doctor instructed Jen as he took his leave.

So, there it was, the romance of the century had begun. What prompted such two unlikely candidates to form an affectionate, bonding partnership is a mystery in human behavior. Explainable or not, it happened. For the next four weeks, Ernest was cared for as though he was a crown prince. The shifts that Jen spent there seemed to make her come alive. Was it her inherent nursing instincts that drew her closer to Ernest? Was it the fact that in her lonely thirty -three years, she had had only one older man friend, a relationship that lasted only six months. That romance, if it could be called a romance, ended when he died suddenly, in her bedroom. The coroner ruled it a natural death from an aneurism.

Before long, Jen would spend slow periods on night shifts chatting with Ernest or reading poetry to him. It was unimaginable that a rough, tough inmate like Ernest was a poetry buff; however, he give Jen that impression and she read classic poems as well as contemporary writings to him.

As the relationship blossomed, Jen learned that Ernest had been raised in a family devoid of love. He had two older brothers that abused him. His father hated him and took every opportunity to ensure Ernest never forgot that fact. At the age of fourteen, Ernest had enough gumption to realize there was more to life then enduring daily beatings. He left home and went to Greenville, the nearest city to his hometown. There he lost himself in the low-income society. It treated him with some dignity and offered him some sense of being. He was befriended by a Salvation Army volunteer, Dave, and they soon became friends. That friendship lasted only a few months, when Dave was arrested for selling drugs, and he received a two-year stretch in a nearby juvenile facility. Disenchanted, Ernest left for Tennessee; or rather, he left and ended up in Tennessee.

Ernest's criminal career began in Spencer. He robbed a gas station; his total take was $43 and a carton of cigarettes. That was considered serious, even though his weapon consisted of a verbal threat, the judge did not take kindly to the young out of state hoodlum. He sentenced Ernest to two years jail time. "I don't want to ever see you in my court again.' Was the judge's stern warning. And he didn't, Ernest headed for Memphis, as soon as he completed his stretch. There he landed a job as a truck swamper, with a company that distributed newspapers and flyers on a contract basis. He would stand on the rear of the delivery van and dash into stores, or fill news lockboxes. Then he would jump back on the van as the driver proceeded to the next stop.

It wasn't exciting work but it paid the bills, well almost paid the bills. Ernest found himself without money on a Saturday night. Two of his hangout friends were in a similar pickle. They walked into a small liquor store and threatened the elderly male employee with harm. One of Ernest's friends had a knife. An off duty police officer promptly arrested the trio, and an armed robbery conviction followed. Ernest received a five-year sentence for his participation in that fiasco, he was out in thirty-nine months.

The next four years were uneventful for Ernest; he worked on a dairy farm with an uncle that thought Ernest had some good somewhere within. Wrong, near the end of those four years Ernest had eyes for his cousin Mary-Jane. Mary-Jane had just turned thirteen and was blossoming like a sunflower in the July sunshine. Ernest thought she was the prettiest gal he had ever laid eyes on. Unfortunately, Ernest now 25 did not stop at merely sight-seeing. He began cozying up to his cousin and soon their deep affection for each other became obvious. After all this was Tennessee in 1985, 'anything goes' was the Cole Porter song still playing regularly in Tennessee.

Well, Ernest soon learned that 'anything goes 'did not resonate with Mary-Jane's father. He took Ernest aside, cuffed him on the side of the head, and read him the riot act, "Son, if you so much as displace a hair on that young filly, you will be hog food, and do you understand me? Mary-Jane is a fine church going little girl and she don't want any more of your hogwash talk about sneaking down to the river with you."

Ernest was all right with that, for a while, and then his anger overcame him. Whom did this dirt farmer think he was ordering around? Ernest had seen more country than they had seen in their fifty years of sod-busting. No one was going to dictate whom he could see and whom he couldn't. He began planning his move. He began saving money from each of his paychecks. He purchased some supplies for his backwoods excursion and he made his escape plan. He kept dropping hints that he would be going into Memphis for a wild weekend at the end of October. His uncle and aunt hearing he would be away, arranged to go on a ninety-mile visit to his aunt's sister. Mary Jane would stay at home and do the chores; however, she would spend the night at the neighbors.

It all sounded so innocent, but Ernest had a different, and as far as he was concerned a better plan. Once her folks were gone, Ernest pounced on Mary Jane, making her accompany him into the Smokey Mountains. For three, lust filled, days he enjoyed the pleasures of Mary Jane's body. Then without hesitation or remorse, he drowned her in the Pigeon River. After burying her body half a mile into the woods, Ernest left for parts unknown.

Mary-Jane's parents reported her missing, citing Ernest as her possible abductor. Within 72 hours, Ernest was apprehended on a bus near Vermont. Presumably, he was hoping to eventually cross the Canadian –USA border into Ontario.

Though a likely suspect in the disappearance of Mary-Jane, the investigators having no evidence, could only encourage him to confess as to his involvement. They appealed to his good nature. He didn't have one!

Finally, a turkey hunter discovered the shallow grave and body of Mary-Jane. A few witnesses remembered seeing Mary-Jane and an older fellow camped near the Pigeon River. After seeing his photo, they readily identified Ernest as the 'older fella'. In musical terms, the jig was up. Ernest had done the whole circuit, from a $43 holdup a few years earlier to a rape and murder conviction. He got twenty years to life in the state penitentiary.

This then was the Ernest that Jen was sharing poetry with, the person she was laughing and joking with. Nice guy or con? That was the question Jen was not asking herself, or she was choosing to ignore.

CHAPTER 2

After four weeks, Ernest had recovered to the extent that he was transferred back to an isolation cell. Fearing another attack against him, he was permitted out in the prison yard for half an hour a day in the accompaniment of a prison guard.

Jen was smitten with Ernest, or so she thought, little difference existed whether her affection was well founded or not. He was her man, and she took each opportunity to visit him. In the first few weeks, as part of her duties, she could check on his condition and tend to his last remaining aches and pains. Then when no more legitimate reasons surfaced, she began to sneak by his cell for a few brief moments to chat and on most visitations bring him some food treats. This did not go unnoticed by both the other inmates, and prison staff. A report was filed by a 'obey the rules' kind of guard and Jen was summoned before the prison board, where they determined she had breached prison rules and guidelines. Their recommendation was for Warden Tom Ames to consider terminating her employment, which he did.

Jen did not regret her actions; she had found her mission in life. It was too simple, she would do everything in her power to get Ernest released. Then she would show him the advantages of life as an honest God-fearing individual who could enjoy life as a husband and the father of her children.

She began her arduous and seemingly insurmountable task. Jen hired a lawyer to review the trial transcripts and supporting evidence. That took several months and he determined that an appeal would not stand any chance of being successful. Jen's only chance to realize her dream of a free Ernest was to encourage him to be a model prisoner and work towards applying for parole. Unfortunately, the earliest Ernest could apply for parole was still seven years away.

Jen couldn't wait that long. Ernest applied to have Jen included on his visitor list. Jen filled out her portion of the application. Within a month, the application was approved. Jen was permitted to visit once a week for two hours. The supervision was stricter than usual, due to the history of the pair. Even hand holding was carefully monitored. The visitation proved frustrating to both Jen and Ernest.

Nine months later, Ernest had an idea, "Let's get married, Honey!" he announced at the beginning of the following week's visitation. It was an unimaginative proposal, but it was music to Jen's ears.

"Darling, you don't know how long I've wanted to marry you. Yes let's get married."

"What do we have to do?"

"There's a form that we fill out and submit to the Warden. Then it's just a matter of a week or two and we can get married right here on the prison grounds. I'll get you started on the form and next week we can fill in my part."

The form was filled out as required; Jen paid the $175 fee, and made an appointment with the Warden's office.

Warden Ames decided to have a serious talk with Jen. "Look Jen, this romance with Ernest, though admirable in some respects is still froth with danger. Are you absolutely certain that you wish to follow through with this marriage?"

Bubbling with excitement, Jen did not hesitate in replying, "Oh yes Warden, Ernest is a good man, he made a mistake in his younger days and I know that is unforgiveable; however, we are soul mates and I will do the utmost to see this through."

"He's still over six years from being eligible for parole, and I must say, I for one will be opposing his application."

"On what grounds?"

"He didn't get that beating last year for being a good guy! In my opinion he is all belt buckle and no herd."

"I disagree, I see many fine qualities in him, he will be a good man after a little TLC."

"I can see you're a determined woman." Warden Ames grabbed a pen and authorized the form allowing the marriage to proceed." He handed it to Jen, "Give this to your clergyman and ask him to contact us for a date that is convenient for you and Ernest." He stood up and extended his hand, "Best of luck to both of you."

Jen, smiling broadly placed the form in her purse "You won't regret this Warden; it's the right thing to do." She walked out of the office beaming like a schoolgirl that just got a date with the school's football quarterback. The difference was that she was not school-girl and Ernest's athletic ability and experience was limited to a few street fights and prison skirmishes.

The Family Visiting Coordinator after talking to Reverend Morris contacted Jen and informed her the wedding was approved to be held in the prison's chapel at 1 p.m. on October 31. Coincidentally the date was Halloween, perhaps a fitting reminder to Jen to be watchful for persons that might do her harm. She ignored the knowing feeling in the pit of her stomach. Ernest was her man, and she was going to have him, and soon.

The date came, the Warden's secretary, who was still friendly with Jen, agreed to be the witness. Jen was dressed in a short skirted wedding gown. Ernest had on the suit that his neighboring cellmate lent him. Reverend Morris did not embellish the ceremony. "Do you, Jen Bristol, take this man, Ernest Hyman, to be your lawfully wedded husband?"

"I do." Jen was shaking with joy. This was the most important day in her 33 years of life.

"Do you, Ernest Hyman, take this woman, Jen Bristol, to be your lawfully wedded wife?"

"I do." Ernest put his arm around Jen to comfort her nervousness.

"If anyone knows of a reason why these two should not be wed, he should come forward now or forever hold their peace."

"A long minute of silence ensued."

Their rings were placed on each other's fingers with the proper ceremonial rhetoric.

The minister concluded, "By the power invested in me, I now

pronounce you husband and wife." He nodded to Ernest to kiss the bride.

He congratulated the happy couple, and motioned them to sign the marriage registry that he had brought with him.

They were married. They were ushered into a private room, where a hired photographer took a few pictures. The guard that had escorted Ernest glanced around the room as if expecting to see someone else present. It was a 10X12 windowless room with a wooden pedestal desk and two chairs. You have fifteen minutes to your selves; I'll knock before entering and wait about two minutes." He turned and left closing the door behind him. Jen and Ernest were finally alone together.

Jen encouraged closeness by stepping forward and cozying up against Ernest. "Well, Honey we've taken the first step in making a life together."

Ernest was only too willing to agree," Thanks for your support Jen, I've never been happier." He held her tight and he began feathering her with kisses. She responded, she knew what was expected of her. Knowing their time was limited she initiated their lovemaking by unbuttoning Ernest's jacket and his shirt, she ran her warm soft hands around his torso and massaged his back with firm yet soothing strokes.

He responded by undoing the zipper on her wedding dress, pulling it up and over her head. Her hands began loosening his belt, his trousers slid down to the floor. He leaned back and lowered himself unto the desk surface, while holding her tight to him. They worked their way back until they were fully covering the desk. The only sound in the room was their breathing as they luxuriated in each other's arms, and bodies. With an eagerness typical of teenagers they rushed to reach the point where they bodies told them they should be. All too soon they were there. Jen knew that this was her destiny; Ernest had brought her out of her stunted womanhood and allowed her to step up and be herself. At last she was a fulfilled woman. They kissed once, then again.

There was a quiet knock on the door. "Five minutes, kids." Was the soft message, who said prison staff weren't considerate?

Jen and Ernest, quickly dressed, Jen rearranged her hair. They both faced the door, just as it opened. "Let's go Honeymooners!" The guard quipped. He gently reached for Ernest's arm and escorted toward the door.

"Ernest, smiled at Jen, thanks Honey, I'll see you next week. Sweet dreams."

Jen blushed and smiled, "I'll be thinking of you." She watched her sweetheart march down the corridor to his prison cell. *I have to get him out of here, she* vowed, as she left the room and departed the building. As she drove homewards, she was listening to Willie Nelson's 'Ladies love Outlaws' C.D.

CHAPTER 3

Three months dragged by, Jen was becoming frustrated with the prison rules that forbade any further 'private time' with her betrothed. Ernest was likewise disenchanted. "Get me out of this hell hole, and I mean sooner than later." He complained as he sat in the visitor's room with glass shielding him from even kissing. They were confined to hand holding and even that was closely monitored. "This isn't human, even animals get affection from one another."

Jen agreed, she had something on her mind, "Ernest, I saw my doctor a few days ago, he has done tests and its official, I am 3 months pregnant. Isn't that wonderful?"

Ernest's face betrayed his feelings; he did not look like a happy expectant father. He sat motionless for a full minute. Then a smile returned to his lips, "Hey, that may help me get an early parole! Good going Jen, I knew you would think of something!" His face was beaming with anticipation, not of a pending newborn, but rather of an opportunity to be free of prison life.

Jen was relived in one way that Ernest was happy about the baby; however, she saw another side of her new hubby. The fact that he might get bonus points towards release seemed to overshadow the joy of starting a family. She rationalized it by telling herself that once he was out his affections and desires for family life would take precedent over his misfortune of being in prison. *He's not a bad guy; he just did one bad thing.* She reassured herself. "I'm glad you're happy Ernest. Yes maybe this will help your case for parole. I'll look into it for us."

Jen contacted the prison administration and was informed in a rather cool manner, " Your pregnancy might have a minimal positive effect on an early release for Ernest, however, the sentencing structure with him was 25 to life and it is unusual to approve early release in such cases."

"Is there anything else that might help him?" Jen was almost frantic. She wanted something more positive to take back to Ernest.

"If he had a guaranteed job waiting for him, now that goes a long way toward an early release, we get a very low reoffender rate on inmates that get immediate employment."

"Well, thank you, that is good news; I'll start working on that!" Jen was buoyed by her advice.

Jen spent the next week canvassing businesses in the surrounding area. A hog farm operation was initially interested, but then backtracked when they were told that Ernest had been convicted of murder. "That puts our other staff at risk, we hire several University students during the summer, and your husband wouldn't fit in with them."

She got the same answer from building contractors, "we might give him some labor jobs now and then but we can't commit to full time, some months we are busy; others we have to lay off our best workers."

She approached the Army recruiting station. "Sorry ma'am, we train soldiers to kill, but they have to be very disciplined in how and when they can kill anyone. Your husband sounds like a bit of a loose cannon, self discipline is lacking in about 50% of our recruit applicants, and we have to weed them out before they either embarrass us or end up causing fatalities because they panic."

She visited Ernest and informed him of her efforts. He was downhearted at the lack of progress. "We have to use some other method! Can you think of any, Honey?"

"She whispered only loud enough for him to hear." Why don't I break you out of here? We can go to Canada, or maybe Alaska, and start over."

Ernest was game, "Let's think about that. I'm due in court next month to testify against those guys who beat me senseless last year. Maybe you can engineer an escape for me, and we can head out."

At first Jen recoiled at the idea, "That would be risking the baby's life and even mine!" She stopped talking as she recalled all the recent negativity she had experienced from the good Christian type community. "Piss on those assholes. I'll get you out, let me know when they transport you over to the courthouse and I'll work out the details."

CHAPTER 4

"Next Wednesday at 12.30 p.m. Ernest quietly informed her. They both knew that he meant that was the time of his being transferred to court..

The guard monitoring their conversation chirped in, "What are you two planning?"

Jen turned and called his bluff, "I'm breaking Ernest here out of prison at 12.30 next week! Don't get in my way buster!"

The guard chuckled as he looked up and down Jen's 110 pound, seven months pregnant frame. "Don't forget to pack the nappies." He chortled. "And be careful the rope ladder doesn't break under you."

"Funny guy" Jen responded with a sexy smile, "I'll bet you're a fun guy when your at home with your wife."

"Never been married, I'm saving myself for the right woman."

"I wish you luck in your single retirement, Jen teased back."

"Your time is up, Honeybunch, pat Mr. Wonderful there good-bye and we'll see you next week, be sure and bring some help with you. On your breakout try."

"It's a date fella." Jen smiled once more and winked at Ernest. "See you, Honey, be on time."

Jen had only 6 days to prepare, and prepare she did. Her tomboy complex resurfaced. She had been an avid hiker, hunter and mark-sperson. She could nail a squirrel in eye at 50 yards. Wiping out a couple of prison security personnel was not the problem. Avoiding the ensuing man-hunters would be the logistical problem. Once she freed Ernest, they would have to move fast, and far. The more distance they put between them and the searchers, the greater their margin of success.

Jen had gotten part time employment with the Happy Valley Rest Home, a scant two miles from the prison. She arranged the rental of a nondescript Volkswagen Rabbit for the initial strike, it would hardly get a second glance. Once she had Ernest on board, they would drive to the rest home and take the manager's GMC Jimmy, the four wheel drive feature of the vehicle would allow them to traverse back country roads.

She stocked up on groceries over a four day period and stowed them in a ravine near the rest home. For a weapon she dug out a .22 caliber Winchester automatic rifle, with a Crossman 4x scope, it was deadly accurate at 50 yards, she thought she would only be about 30 yards from her targets. She loaded the magazine with fifteen long rifle hollow point bullets. On impact they would shatter and do severe tissue damage to anyone or anything that was in its' path of fire. A shot through a jam can would make a pencil size entry wound and a 4 inch exit hole as it shattered and flew out the far side of the can. She fitted a simple silencer to the muzzle.

She arranged to purchase several used men's clothing sets, of pants, shirt, and socks. That together with an all season jacket and rugged hiking boots would gave her and Ernest an edge if they were forced into the backwoods.

CHAPTER 5

I t was 12 noon on Wednesday, everything was set. Jen parked her V.W.Rabbit near the gate that led from the prison yard to the service vehicle parking lot. The routine she had remembered in such instances was always the same. Two unarmed security personnel would escort their prisoner in shackles through the prison gate to a waiting van driven by another armed security person. For further security the guards in the corner towers had kept watch on vehicles arriving and leaving. The stage was set, Jen was almost out of the vision line of the nearest tower, the second one was 300 feet from her position.

A laundry truck left the prison yard, behind it Jen could see three men walking toward the gate, one of them was in orange prison overalls and shackled, it was Ernest. They walked through the gate, which closed remotely behind them, the driver of the van stepped down and walked around front of the van to open the sliding side door. Jen took a bead on his forehead and squeezed off a round. The man dropped in a heap, his brain matter was gushing out with the spurting blood.

Ernest, seeing the action had started, swung his manacled arms sideways to his left sending one security man flying, then in a reverse swinging motion he swung his arms the other way, catching the other guard in the shoulder and dropping him cold. Ernest was free of their clutches. He moved as quickly as he could toward the V.W. Rabbit, Jen was already in it and driving toward him. The V.W. passenger door swung open and he literally fell into the front seat as Jen accelerated away from the scene. The tower men, fired a few futile shots at the speeding vehicle without hitting a vital engine part, or either Jen or Ernest.

"Nice work Honey. What's next?"

"We're switching vehicles about a mile up the road, crouch down if you can, we don't want people spotting your tunic."

In less than two minutes they were piling into the GNC Jimmy, Jen drove to the ravine cache of supplies and in sixty seconds loaded them in the back of the Jimmy.

It had been a masterfully planned escape. They had at least a five- minute lead and that meant the prison already had a twenty five square mile of real estate to consider. Jen drove down the interstate for four minutes, and fearing roadblocks might be set up ahead, she took a lesser grid road heading northwest toward Illinois hoping to continue north into Canada.

"Ernest was impatiently trying to wiggle out of the nylon hand restraints and finally managed to get one hand free." There's a hunting knife here on my belt" she barked. "Get that other hand free and start cutting you tunic off, I have some clothes in the back."

"What about the leg irons?"

"We'll stop and cut the chain part off, up ahead. The irons around your legs have to stay on for now, that's a two hour job to saw through them."

"You're good?" Ernest couldn't help but admire the spunkiness of his new partner,

"I know," was her cute reply. She couldn't believe they had been able to get away without any serious challenges. She realized they were now fugitives wanted for murder, she thought back. *Could she have spared the guard his life? Not likely, it was him or the two of them, there are no half measures when your life is in the balance. You do whatever it takes.*

She saw an abandoned farm that sported a shop building, "We'll stop up here at the shop, it could be that a farmer still stores tools here when he comes out to plant his crops." She drove around to the back of the shop, hiding the GMC from the roadway. "We can get out and have a look." They walked up to the door of the shop and Ernest kicked in the flimsy clapboard lower part of the door and Jen reached up and unlocked the doorknob.

They found a steel chisel and a heavy hammer and began forcing open the leg irons. After several blows there was some give and soon Ernest was free of the restraints.

Jen had gotten some clothes, here put these on while I hide the prison stuff, she grabbed up everything and flung it all down a 40 foot dry well a few yards from the shed. They heard a police siren out on the road and they peeked around the corner in time to see the vehicle going toward the way they had just left. "They think they can head us off, that's good we are past their initial roadblock, now e can put some real distance behind us."

CHAPTER 6

It was only two o'clock as they left the grid road and turned northward on an interurban highway, the traffic was fairly heavy and there were no signs of roadblocks or slowdowns. Jen let Ernest drive, "Just head north, don't speed and turn off at the first sign of a major slowdown in the traffic pattern." She instructed him.

Ernest couldn't believe his good fortune, he was free! They had some money, a vehicle and he had someone who believed in him. He was utterly flabbergasted that Jen would kill to free him. Now if that wasn't true love what was it? He made a mental note not to ever get her riled up, not as long as that squirrel gun was within her reach! He was feeling groovy as they sped down the highway, the radio blaring music and the late fall weather crisp. An hour later with no sign of pursuers it was evident they had outmaneuvered the lawmen. Ernest saw an economy motel up the road, "Honey why don't we stop for a few hours and get some rest." His idea of rest was not without some added pleasures.

"Jen, thought for a moment. "Ernest, I would be all for that, however, we are still risking being caught if we stop. Now don't get me wrong, I want to stop as much as you do. " She reached for a roadmap and began studying it. She looked up and smiled, I think we can take a break. There's a fishing resort on the lake ahead with some cabins. We can crash in a cabin for a couple of hours, and then keep on going. How about that?

"Sounds like a good plan!" Ernest was okay with that, he sped up a few more mph and envisioned how dreamy the next couple of hours could be for him and Jen.

"Stop here!" Jen hollered as they went back to the last row of cabins on the lake.

"That's a wreck of a place!" Ernest replied, "My cell was more attractive than that."

"That's the point, no one would expect us to camp out in a place like that!"

"I see, there is method to your madness! Okay let's pile out and check into the Honeymoon Suite" They stopped behind the run-down building, grabbed some food and sleeping bags and went inside, through a window, of course.

"Welcome home Ernest!" Exclaimed Ernest, as he saw a fairly well kept interior staring back at him. "This will do" he said to Jen. They put down their packs and bags and Jen began preparing a meal. " Come here Honey, we have better things to do then eat! Let's live on love for a while."

"I'm all for that, but we have to keep an eye on the time." Jen joined him on the sofa. They were beginning to feel comfortable and relaxed when they heard a voice call out. "Who's in there?"

Jen jumped up readjusted her clothing and went to the front door, picked up some mail on the floor and opened the door. "Looking, for someone?" She asked the seventy something elderly looking lady.

"Mr. Grilz always asks me to check on anyone around his place."

Jen made a quick reply, oh, didn't Uncle Harry call you, he told me to expect you to check on us. Come in, we are newly weds and having a honeymoon on a shoestring budget, that is why Uncle Harry said we could spend the night here, we're going East to California", she lied.

"Oh, I'm ever so sorry for intruding! I should know better. No dearie I won't come in, perhaps I'll see you in the morning? She turned to leave. I'm two houses down if you need anything."

"Thanks ma'am, that's mighty neighborly of you." Jen closed the door, and they both began laughing. "I wish everyone was that Gullible!"

"How did you know the guy's name was Harry?"

"The mail, I looked down and saw the name, Harry Grilz, so I just added uncle."

"Clever girl!" Ernest reached for her, " Where were we sweetheart?"

"Where ever you think you should be, let's get it on before we have anymore interruptions, just be careful of our baby."

"Baby won't be upset, guaranteed, I know how to take it nice and easy, after all this is Tina Turner country."

"You're Simply the Best "Jen murmured as they reveled in the joys of lovemaking.

CHAPTER 7

Several hours later, Jen was awakened by the sound of voices and flashing lights, police car lights. It was not their day after all, a mega phone message was directed to them. Jen Bristol and Ernest Hyman, this is the Tennessee State police, you are surrounded. Please come out through the front door with your hands in plain view. You have three minutes to comply.

"Shit!" Ernest exclaimed, what happened?

"We took too long, obviously the neighbor lady must have seen my picture on T.V as you know the prison has all the staff photos. We were dupes and we were duped. This is the end of the line, let's go out there before they come in here and hurt the baby."

"Hurt the baby! Is that only fucking thing you think about? Where is your gun, I'll take a few of these bastards with me before I'll give myself up!"

"The rifle is in the GMC. Come on dear, let's say we gave it a good try, now it's over don't swim upstream, they'll kill us all. Don't forget we killed a security officer."

You go ahead. I'm looking for another way out of this mess. I'm not going back to that hell hole of a prison."

"You have no choice. Unless you can vaporize yourself out of here like Mr. Spock you are as screwed as I am. We are going to prison and that is a certainty." Jen started for the door, opening it she called out I'm coming out don't shoot, I'm seven months pregnant for God's sake, don't shoot us."

"Just step out on the porch and then move to your right ma'am; you'll be alright."

Jen moved forward and was crossing the threshold when she felt a tremendous blow strike her on the back between her shoulder blades. The pain was excruciating, as she was falling forward and blacking out she heard Ernest's voice swearing at her. "You bitches are all the same, you get what you want and then you throw us men to the wolves. I'm sick of the lot of you, he swung the axe again and it came down hard striking the porch floor right alongside Jen's belly, he had been trying to kill the baby. A hail of gunfire shattered the country air as the order to fire was given. Ernest was blown backward and was dead before his body made contact with the wooden floor.

The policemen rushed forward, with guns drawn, they saw there would be no further need. The Sergeant barked an order to the officer in the police car, " Get an ambulance attendants up here, we have a baby to save!" The Sergeant knelt down beside Jen, and felt a weak pulse. "You'll be okay, Ma'am, we'll save you and the baby, just hang on now, you hear?" He knew he was only half-right.

The ambulance personnel knelt down and began attaching life support tubes to Jen, " I think we can make it to the village hospital, tell them we'll be there in about five minutes. The baby girl was delivered a few minutes after they laid Jen out on the operating table, her vital signs flat lined, and she was taken off life support.

The nurse cuddled the little bundle, "what a start for a little angel. What name shall we use on the records here?"

The delivery Doctor, looked at the police report and replied," use 'Baby Bristol', this child does not deserve to be in anyway associated with the name Ernest Hyman."

"What should we enter under the father's name?"

"Father unknown."

The End

THE PERFECT
CHILD

CHAPTER 1

"I regret to have to inform you folks. It's unlikely that you will be able to conceive a child." Doctor Neilson looked up from his file to see what his patients' reaction would be. Not that he didn't know what to expect. As a fertility specialist, he had been through this many times.

Rob and Linda Flett, his patients, were devastated, "Are you certain?"

"Let's say 99 %, there is always the possibility of a minor miracle."

"So then, we can definitely forget about having a child?" Rob looked disheartened.

"You can always adopt, or wait a few years; things are changing every month in genetics research and other aspects of human reproduction, who knows what's around the bend."

"Are you referring to a test-tube baby? I thought that was a subject confined to science fiction?" Linda questioned.

"Not any more! We are on the verge of breaking through on the science of human cloning. This is October 2002. I would expect that the world will see a cloned baby before 2003. You've no doubt heard about the English group who cloned 'Dolly" the sheep?"

Rob, recalled "Yes, that was a 1997 headline news. Are we that close to cloning a human?"

"I would speculate that we are closer than we think! Companies have a way of delaying progress reports to gain a marketing advantage over competitors. However, check out the information wherever you can, the library, the internet, and so on. Then visit me in six months. We will see what has developed by that time."

As Rob and Linda were driving home, Linda was skeptical, "Rob did you think he was making us feel better by exaggerating cloning?"

"It's interesting, we are in our thirties and we may very well see some interesting things in the next few years. Technology has a way of bursting ahead as it advances."

"Would you consider cloning?"

Rob laughed, "Imagine me walking around and having five little copies of myself running after me like ducklings after their mother!"

Linda laughed at the mental image, "Let's get serious, why not consider cloning, if it's available? You're a nuclear scientist; I'm a concert violinist and we have the right genes to produce the perfect child."

"That was our plan, but in cloning, only the one individual gets reproduced, it's not a joint effort like a normal pregnancy."

"Perhaps we can take your cells and modify them to eliminate the defective genes and then insert some of my superior genes. Then we would have a perfect baby, a boy of course, because he would have 90% or more of your cell makeup." She continued as her imagination spark by her high I.Q. explored the alternatives. We can each have our cells modified and then cloned. That's it we will produce two superior children, one cloned from you, and the other from me. Two superior children ready to take on the world, either as a pair or individually."

"An intriguing idea, let's do a feasibility study on that. I have three months of leave coming. I can take it now and we can delve deeply into this 'genetics and cloning' subject."

Linda could hardly contain herself "We'll have a perfect child. I know we will. I have that old fashioned woman's intuitive feeling."

CHAPTER 2

Rob, filed for a leave of absence which his employer, a crown corporation of the federal Government, readily accepted. They were between major research jobs and could spare Rob for a few months.

Linda had some concert performances, but they would still allow her to assist Rob with research and data organization. The stage was set.

They redecorated the room, that had been intended for a baby, and turned it back into an office and then they set up two computers on desks, file cabinets and an assortment of periphery equipment.

The first exciting news they uncovered was a news item about the first human cloned in December of that year, the baby aptly named Eve, was born by caesarean section, the technique parroted those used for Dolly the Sheep . The company divulged they had four other expectant mothers expecting cloned babies.

Linda was overjoyed, "It's just a matter of months and this cloning business will go commercial."

"You may be right!" Rob didn't want to dampen Linda's expectations: however, in his own mind he thought it might be years before they could expect help with their plans.

A few months later, Rob saw there was a symposium on cloning in New York. He pulled in a few favors and was nominated to the delegation his government was sending. There were four of them, all experts in their field. It would be an excellent chance for the Fletts, to advance their plans and be among the first couples to be selected. Linda was to accompany Rob and organize the notes and information that flowed out of the symposium.

The information was extensive, if not always on the topic of human cloning; nevertheless, all the information could be reworked to make it feasible for the human procedures.

First, there was a presentation on cloning from frozen tissue, a mouse that had been frozen for sixteen years had been successfully cloned. The questions raised were more of the ethical and practical nature asking the one present question *"should we be even be considering doing this?"*

Secondly, there was a day spent on 'Designer babies' by using genetic engineering methods. Again, the ethical issues surfaced. Since parents all want a perfect child physically, mentally and of the sex of their preferred choice, this presentation was of immense interest to Rob. He made accurate and copious notes on everything said, he took all the handout information sheets available. He knew they would of enormous interest to Linda.

Another evening session covered the ethical dilemma of choosing the sex of the clone subject. The general consensus was that financial responsible would-be-parents would be the best judge on the child they wished to produce, and how it would be raised to become a contributing member of society.

Yet, other subjects covered emotional needs of people that wished to be cloned the same sex parent issue arose, as always in any parenting situation, and the controversial subject of cloning a human to harvest replacement parts for the parents or siblings drew the most discussion from the 'ethical crowd' section. Finally, the topic covered the stance of the Human Fertilization and Embryology Authority, and the Human Genetics Advisory Commission, who had approved the concept human cloning in cases of cloning for therapeutic purposes. It did, however, stop short of approving cloning to make babies genetically identical to their parents. As the debates continued there was a shift pointing the way for a revising of the rules to permit cloning of babies.

The raw facts did, however, point to a few pitfalls, there was a high rate of failure in the cloning process. The clone usually was much larger and had larger organs that the original. It was more susceptible to immune deficiencies, prone to an earlier death and often had difficulties adapting to social situations, feeling like an outsider.

Armed with several boxes of material, the Fletts returned home buoyed by the fact that there would soon be an opportunity for couples to volunteer to become 'test' subjects.

Their chance came a year later, a progressive company in Helsinki had reached the point of commencing cloning for 'a few select clients.' Rod's name had been gleaned by the firm from the attendee list of the New York symposium, of interested persons. The information transmitted to Linda and Rob following their application, was detailed in its questions. It was obvious the main drive was to produce 'super babies' not the everyday hit and miss variety that people were producing naturally.

CHAPTER 3

After three months of evaluation and testing, Linda and Rob, were notified to appear before the selection committee for a final interview. The committee was made up of four individuals. Trevor Hill CEO of Dynamic Cloning Inc., his Vice president Nancy Gray, the company 's head of the cloning division, Doctor Norman Sealmann, and of course the company lawyer, Sven Dirikison.

The boardroom on the 44th floor of the office building looked out over the city. It was a bright sunny May afternoon. Trevor Hill, was the first to speak, " Our first and perhaps only main concern is that the subjects of our test group are totally devoted to the project, if I can use that term. Of course being even more devoted to one another is the next requirement. The baby we will assist you in producing must have the best of these environment and stability factors. That will ensure that he or she will develop to his or her full potential. To do so otherwise would taint the results of the test.

Of the twenty sets of applicants, you two have scored the highest. I'll turn the floor over to Nancy Gray our Vice President, she's an experienced geneticist.

Nancy Gray opened her file, "We have determined that we would clone Mr. Flett first. He exhibits a higher intelligence." She turned and looked at Linda, "Don't take what I'm saying as a negative, Mrs. Flett, we work with the easiest subject first. We have determined we will enhance the baby's musical and artistic talents by replacing those genetic markers of your husband, with those of yours. We will also modify the genetic structures with your superior facial and body attributes, in other words, make a more attractive baby."

Doctor Sealmann, will be in charge of the technical and operational aspects, you will be working with him more closely than with any of us other board members. Now, I'll turn our legal beagle loose, Sven Dirikison, if you please."

"Thank you, Miss Gray, now there are some aspects of our contract that you have to understand fully, they are as follows," he glanced at his file, "This child will be yours, and you will be responsible for the acceptance of it in whatever form it arrives."

"Do you mean if it is mentally retarded?"

"Yes, not only that, and I don't wish to alarm you, but we are venturing into the fringes of the unknown. There is a small, perhaps even remote chance that, to use an everyday phrase, 'the plane may crash' in plain language an imperfect child could result. During the gestation period, we will be testing and observing regularly all signs, to ensure there are no abnormalities. If there are sufficient reasons to consider it, abortion, may be recommended. That will be your personal choice, if it ever comes to that. Do you understand that clause?"

"Yes, it is our choice to make an informed decision to continue if anything untoward pops up."

"The project will be completely secret. It will be our sole right to divulge when and how much information, if any, is reported to the authorities or the news media or any other group. We will also have an exclusive right, copyright if you wish, to use the child as a test subject, as a source on new cloning material, but only if we do no harm to the child."

'So you will, in effect, own our child?" Rob was feeling uneasy.

"Not own it, just have limited access to it for further work, the child would be our 'pattern' for producing the same or similar children."

"Will all these children generally have the same appearance, like the sheep and mice that we have read about?"

"Yes, it's almost like a photo-copy except for the introduced genes added, or lacking the ones removed."

"When do you propose to start?"

"Today, you sign our contract. Then in a month we begin the actual cloning process."

Linda, was eager to begin, "Let's sign now, I want this baby!"

Rob, tried to reason with her, "Look dear this should be discussed, we'll discuss it overnight and come in tomorrow to finalize the contract." He turned to Dirikison, "May I have a copy of the contract document?"

"Why not?" He handed Bob two copies. "I'll see you tomorrow."

"You probably will," Rob agreed, as Linda ushered him out of the room."

CHAPTER 4

Linda began the discussions as they were driving homeward. "Why did you stop us from signing Rob?

"This is a serious matter, I think we have to reflect on all the information we were given back there."

"Which ones bother you?"

"Access to our child for further research, is the main one."

"They will only use minute samples, the child will not be harmed."

"That's what they say now, but down the road, these contracts can be interpreted in different ways to justify most actions."

"They are trusting us, we have to trust them."

"I still don't like it! Now, how about you? Was there anything you felt uncomfortable with?"

"Just the comment, that we are on the cutting edge of this technology and that there may be some unforeseen consequences."

"Sure, it's a gamble in part, but someone has to lead the way."

"I suppose, you're right, nothing is guaranteed, and they will be monitoring my condition closely."

Rob replied, "Since I'm first, the success of you with the next child should be even less problematic, they will have had the experience of doing the first child."

"Then we'll do it," Linda was pushing for a positive answer.

"Sure, I'm ready we both want a child or children, and even if it isn't a 'super baby' we will still have a baby of our own. That should be our first desire; a perfect child is secondary."

That evening the stress of the day's events wore away and Linda and

Rob relaxed by celebrating by having a two person wine and cheese party. By 10 p.m. the merrymaking had made its way to the bedroom. Linda and Rob could now make love freely, without the stress of having sex at the right time, in the best position and worrying about what might or might not happen. It had been three years now that they had been aware of fertility problems.

"Now, we can do it for our selves!" Linda cooed as they joined together for the final minutes of sexual enjoyment.

"Isn't this something!" Rob agreed as they reveled in each other's arms. "This is fantastic, don't stop ever."

"You're a tiger tonight!" Linda exclaimed as she joined wholeheartily in their efforts to reach a simultaneously high.

Their unbridled enthusiasm drove their pleasure to new heights, starlight flashes erupted in their minds as they totally lost themselves in each other. 'Now!" Linda screamed as she slipped into ecstasy.

Rob responded as never before, "Now that was something!" He whispered after they held each other for what seemed like a gloriously long time.

"Wow and wow!' Linda exclaimed as she loosened her hold on Rob. "Take me there again!"

The partying continued into the night.

Sven Didrikson was jovial as the Fletts joined him in his office. "I assume you are planning to seal the deal?"

Linda blushed at the mental image she still had from the previous night, she thought, *we already sealed the deal last night*; however she replied. "Yes. Mr. Didrikson, we are ready to sign the contract and proceed with the cloning."

The papers were reviewed with them once more and then they signed.

"Now ,I'll send you to Nancy she does the preliminary work for Dr. Sealmann.

They were directed to Nancy Gray's office, it was next to a medical clinic-like lab.

After meeting and welcoming them into her office, she explained the plan. "I'll give you an appointment schedule and after a couple of visits here, After that there is an incubation period for the clone, after which, you Mts. Flett, will be will scheduled for the implantation. That will be about two months from now. After that it will be like a normal pregnancy, the only exception will be some extra testing, as we discussed with you yesterday."

"I can't believe this is happening!" Linda was so thrilled to be finally able to have her wishes for a child fulfilled.

"Believe it, it is, and I see you are most pleased." She turned to Rob, "and you Mr. Flett, are you excited as well?"

" Yes, ma'am, I may not show it like 'mommy' here, but yes indeed, this is what we have been waiting for, to start a family."

"Perfect, now come in a week from today and we will take the necessary tissue samples from each of you, and the process will begin."

It was a glorious day as Linda and Rob drove the twenty minutes to their apartment.

"I have a concert rehearsal later this afternoon Rob, would you mind driving me, it's faster that the subway."

"No problem. I'll make notes on everything that has happened in the last few days, I may write a book about our experiences."

"Surely, but not about last night? Promise?"

"Promise. I'll only use it if it comes into play in the novel?"

"How could it?" Linda was sure it would not be relevant in any way.

CHAPTER 5

Two months later

Linda got a phone call from Nancy Gray "We are ready to proceed with the implantation. Come into our clinic tomorrow at 8 a.m. and you will undergo a final examination. Then if that is all in order, we will proceed with the implantation. You'll be here for over five hours so I would suggest that Mr. Flett drop you off and come back after that time. It's rather boring sitting in a waiting room for five hours."

"8 a.m. great I'll be there!" Linda was ecstatic, the time had arrived. She called Rob in from his workshop, where he was in the process of building a crib for the baby's nursery. "I'm to go to the clinic tomorrow morning, they suggested you drop me off and come back later because it will take several hours."

"Fine, I have to go to the office. I start work again next week; have them call me there when you are ready to come home."

Linda arrived and began receiving a few routine tests. She was readied and asked to wait to proceed to the operating room. Her private room was devoid of any windows or artwork, it was a simple bed with one chair and a small bathroom. *Even an outhouse has more ambience than this,* she thought as she read the one tattered Women's Day magazine, that had been left behind by some other patient.

Nancy Gray, came in about a half an hour later. "Sorry we took so long, we had to double check one of your tests."

"Is something wrong?" Linda could see the quizzical look on Nancy's face.

"You might say something is right Mrs. Flett, the urine test we did on you, indicated that you are two months pregnant!"

"Really! " Linda stood up, a look of amazement covered her face. "Are you certain? We were told there was only a remote chance of that happening!"

"It's true, we've seen this before. As soon as a couple stop worrying about conceiving a baby, they relax and it takes place, nature goes to work. That is what obviously happened here."

Linda remembered the wine and cheese party they had on the night they decided to go ahead on the cloning. "I know when it happened!" She happily smiled, then turned serious.

" What about the test tube baby, what will happen to it?"

"You have four options; however we should call your husband first, then Dr. Sealmann will discuss the choices with both of you. You can decide on the one that best suits you."

"Rob, are you sitting down?" Linda asked when Rob's secretary connected him.

"Yes, I am, what's wrong?"

"I'm pregnant." Linda announced.

"That's what I took you down there for, are you joking?"

"No, Honey, I am naturally pregnant, I'm two months along."

Rob grasped the reality of her remarks. "Say, that's great!"

"Well, yes and no, we have to decide how we are going to proceed with the test-tube baby. They want you to come down and we will have our options explained to us."

"I seems simple, cancel everything else, we are having our own baby."

"Just a minute Rob, stay on the line." Linda repeated his message to Nancy. Then again turned and spoke to Rob. "They want you to come down. It's more complicated than you say."

Rob, began to visualize the dynamics of the situation. "Sure, I'll be there in about twenty minutes."

Dr. Sealmann, walked into Nancy Gray's office were she and both Linda and Rob were waiting. "We have choices here folks. Now, don't react until I go through the options. We are here to guide you, and the decision you make will be yours and yours alone.

"This can unfold like this, you can proceed with your normal pregnancy. I wouldn't think you would want to do anything else but that so we won't go there. Now, as far as the embryo that is ready for implantation there you have three choices." He paused, then continued. " We can freeze it and save it in case you need it. We can destroy it right now or later once, you have your baby. Finally, you can implant it in a surrogate mother and have a second child within a month of the natural one you are now carrying."

Rob looked at Linda, and she looked at him, it was obvious this would take some thought. Rob spoke first, "Leave us alone for a few minutes and Linda and I will see if we are thinking the same way on this."

"Come on Nancy, its coffee time," Dr. Sealmann helped her up and they left the Fletts to ponder their dilemma.

"Well Rob, do you understand the choices?"

"Quite clearly, I say we forget destroying the embryo!"

Linda nodded "I agree."

"Now, I think the surrogate idea should be considered. The point is, do we do it now, or wait a year ? How do you feel about raising what amounts to twins?"

"With some help from a nanny, which we can easily afford, I have no problem with that. In fact, I think we have solved the problem. The clinic gets to proceed and we get a second child."

"We may end up with two boys."

"That's fine they are still both ours. Isn't this a wonderful development? We get the best of both worlds. Go find Nancy and Doctor Sealmann."

Rob told them of their choice as they re-entered the office. Dr.Sealman was pleased, we'll get a surrogate from our list of willing applicants. I want you to meet her. Quite often they wish to remain as an 'aunt' to the child she helped bring into the world."

"That sounds reasonable, yes, have her contact us and we'll meet."

CHAPTER 6

One evening, two days later, they received a phone call, "I'm Marg O'Brien, Doctor Sealmann referred me to you."

Linda responded, "Yes, we were waiting for your call.' She continued, "Rob my husband and I would like to meet with you. What is a good day for you?"

"Tomorrow is Saturday, that suits me."

"Us too, can you meet us for lunch, at Mino's in the Orchard Park shopping center? Say at 11.30?"

"Perfect, I'm only ten minutes from there. My phone number here is 204-433-4652 if there are any changes. I'm a tall, blonde, woman, 38, and I'll be carrying a red purse."

"We're looking forward to meeting you, Marg."

"As am I, I want to meet the pair of you!"

❦

Marg, was a charming individual, she had worked as a teacher in the high school system for ten years. She was married and raising her two children now six and eight years of age. Rather than go back to work and have to deal with daycare she had done one surrogate job, and was willing to do another. "I can spend time with my kids, and help you out as well, we both win."

Rob had only one concern, "Health wise how do you rate?"

"Oh, I'm very robust, I jog daily, we ride bikes on weekends, I don't drink excessively, perhaps one drink a week ,I'm a non smoker, and I'm not on any medication at all. The clinic insists on moderation in all things and no smoking, drugs or powerful meds. Only 15% of applicants manage to meet their standards!"

Rob sat back and began to listen to Marg and Linda discuss pregnancy issues, delivery dangers, and related topics. He began to see the real Marg emerge, as a caring, loving, highly intelligent woman. Those traits added to her simple natural beauty made Rob begin to imagine the unthinkable. As the conversation turned to more general topics, Rob leaned forward and joined in. He was stimulated by Margi's comprehension of everything from politics, to world affairs, even to her choices of menu items.

Marg sensing his keen admiration and interest, responded to his interaction and soon the flow of conversation had shifted 180 degrees from Linda and Marg, to Marg and Rob.

Now it was Linda who sat back and wondered just how the evening would end. She decided to hasten the end of the meeting. Looking at her watch, she interrupted the other two. " Rob, we have to go soon, I have to attend a rehearsal this evening."

Rob, knowing there was no rehearsal, played along with the ruse. "Of course, Darling." He motioned the server to the table and requested the check. Then he turned to face Marg, "It was a pleasure meeting you Marg, I'm sure the clinic will be in touch with you soon."

Linda, nodded somewhat reluctantly, as though not that sure about Margi's suitability, or rather about the fact she was too suitable to Rob. "Yes, Marg, it was a joy to meet you, and thank you for the tips on pregnancy management, I'm sure I will benefit from them." They stood up as the server brought the bill.

Marg, was most gracious, "I'm very pleased to be considered as your surrogate, and am looking forward to the experience." She smiled broadly; her eyes were focusing on Rob.

Linda was somewhat cool toward Rob, "Did you have to warm up to her like that? I was embarrassed watching the two of you embracing each other with your eyes."

"I'll admit she is an interesting, and even alluring person; but believe me Honey she will only be a necessary part of our life for eight months. After that we will not see very little of her, she'll go on to other things and you and I will have a family to raise. There is no ulterior motive here. Why not go with someone who is compatible and friendly. Would you rather have some grouchy, misfit as your surrogate?"

"I'm not so sure I want Marg. What if she causes legal problems by not giving us the baby?"

"I'm certain, that's all covered in a contract, she provides the service, she gets paid, end of contract!"

"I want a legal opinion on what rights she may be able to claim."

"I looked into that already, and since we are not using her egg then she has no claims whatsoever."

"I'm nervous about all this!"

"Would you rather wait a year, and then do the second child yourself? I'm sure the clinic can wait."

Linda relaxed, "No, let's do it now, I want both babies to grow up together."

Rob settled the discussion "Then it's agreed, we use Marg."

Linda nodded, without saying anything further.

Seven Months Later

"It's a girl!" the Doctor announced to Rob, as the baby was delivered. Linda's pregnancy had gone well, there were no complications and the proof was there in a kicking and screaming 9-pound daughter.

"Darling, we have a girl!" Rob repeated to Linda, who was beginning to unwind after a moderately difficult delivery.

A wide smile lit up her face, "Let me see her." She wanted her baby.

The nurse, who had just finished cleaning the baby wrapped her in a blanket and placed her in her mother's arms. "Congratulation, here is your daughter Mommy. Have you chosen a name yet?"

Linda cuddled the little bundle of life and looking down admiring the delicate features of the youngster, cooed. "The name we picked is Phyllis, it's a Greek name meaning sweetheart or country girl, for a second name we picked Melody.

"Phyllis Melody Flett, that sounds very fitting for a musician's daughter."

It was the happiest day of their lives for both Linda and Rob. Their dreams of being parents were coming true.

One Month Later

"It's a son!" Dr. Sealmann announced to Rob and Linda as he emerged from the clinic's delivery room. "He's a fine looking little fella, 10 pounds five ounces. You have the start of a healthy youngster there." He paused, "We will keep him here for two days to ensure everything is functioning. Then you can take him home to meet your daughter."

"How often do we have to report back to you?" Rob enquired.

"Once every six months, similar to normal babies. In addition, once he's five perhaps once a year to track his physical development, and mental aptitude . The fact that you have a natural baby to use as a comparative will give us invaluable data for our evaluations. "

"You mean we have to bring Phyllis Melody in as well?" Linda was surprised.

"Not legally, but it would be a unique opportunity to compare their growth. Think about it and let me know what you decide."

Two days later little Vincent, Roger Flett, as he was named was sharing the nursery in the Flett household. The first two months were busy ones as the Flett's adjusted their routines to accommodate the babies' needs. Linda had taken a two-year leave of absence from the orchestra. Rob was able to work a thirty-hour week with flexible hours.

The first 6-month evaluation was due, both Rob and Linda had agreed to take advantage of the clinic's offer to do a comparative evaluation of their children. They talked to Nancy Gray, while Dr.Sealmann was examining Phyllis and Vincent. "Have you noticed any peculiarities or differences in your youngsters, that may be of value in our study?"

Linda answered first," I seem to have bonded with Phyllis very well, she is seeking attention and interaction, even at this young age. Vincent is more withdrawn and content to occupy himself with visual items like his mobile at first and then his plastic toys and colorful blocks. When Phyllis crawls over to him, he doesn't share anything with her. Phyllis cries quickly, Vincent rarely cries."

"You bonded with Phyllis in part due to your breast feeding. However, it is not unusual for some babies to be 'loners,' a small percentage, maybe 20% will exhibit that independent nature. As far as the crying is concerned, that is not unusual, Vincent is more hardnosed and is not prone to crying."

She turned to Rob, "As their father, do you notice the same reaction when you hold the children?"

Rob nodded. " For sure, Phyllis is a little angel wanting to be held and cuddled, in fact we have nicknamed her 'Cuddles,' Vincent is more thrilled with games of motion, as being swung in a semi arc up and down, he enjoys the scary sensations. He also seems to be continually figuring mentally how things are put together and how they roll or bounce or slide."

"Those are you scientist's genes at play there, that all seems normal and expected." Nancy hesitated, "You wait here and I will go and assist Dr.Sealmann, we'll have the children back to you in a few minutes."

Nancy Gray entered the examination room, Dr.Sealmann was watching the children interact with various toys and articles in a large padded playpen. He turned to face Nancy, "What did they tell you?"

"That same characteristic of aloofness is being exhibited by the cloned boy, as we had in about seventy-five percent of our cases."

"Yes, I can see that here there is a lack of innocence in the boy, the little girl is all smiles and giggles; he is serious, methodical and aloof, -almost robotic!"

"Robotic sounds like a pretty harsh word to apply to a six month old!"

"Perhaps' unemotional 'would be a better word, I'll use that in my report. Now, did anything else come up, in your discussion with the parents?"

"The boy likes daring, scary swings through the air, better than close hugs and the like."

"His brain seeks adventures and challenges, he's looking for new experiences. That's good we have a smarty developing here." Here let's take the children back to the parents, I'll do the talking." Dr. Sealmann picked up Vincent, and Nancy Gray picked up Phyllis and they walked back to the interview room. "Here are your cuties." Dr.Sealman handed Vincent to Rob, while Nancy returned Phyllis to Linda's outstretched arms. They are both coming along fine, and they are definitely two different kids."

"Is there any need to be concerned Doctor?" Linda asked nervously.

"Not at all, as time goes on they will change. Everything is new and how they react now and a year from now to situations could be quite different. They are healthy, you are doing a good job of keeping them active, just keep on and we will see you in another six months." He smiled warmly to reassure Linda and Rob everything was normal.

CHAPTER 7

V incent began walking at nine months, Phyllis at eleven months . Vincent exhibited more aggressive and controlling behavior towards Phyllis, to the point where Linda had to ensure she was present when the children were playing together. By the time Vincent was one year old he was exhibiting behavior that was verging on abnormal. The Fletts reported this to the clinic on Vincent's one-year evaluation.

"Dr. Sealmann attempted to explain the behavior . " I can say that even though his aggressiveness is somewhat unusual, it is still not abnormal. Siblings in all of nature have a survival trait that puts them in a 'me first' mode, whether it's to get their share of food , shelter or warmth."

"So then, we have nothing to worry about?" Rob answered.

"Other than to ensure he doesn't inadvertently injure Phyllis, let them interact as normal. Perhaps Phyllis will develop a defensive attitude and fight back. In the meantime, exert a little discipline in Vincent's case , so he learns there are boundaries to his behavior. It will take some effort, but he will get the message. With his high intelligence, he may just modify his manner rather quickly, to avoid the discipline."

Later that evening the Flett family was in the living room enjoying playtime prior to the kid's bedtime. Vincent was deliberately heaving blocks toward Phyllis. One block hit her on the shoulder and she began to cry. Vincent was smiling and preparing to pick up a second block. Rob interrupted by grabbing his hand and giving it a swift whack and simultaneously saying "no." Vincent instead of crying, proceeded to pick up the block and threw it at Rob." Okay young fellow." Rob spanked his bottom with a light blow. Then he picked him up, took Vincent into the nursery, putting him in his crib and covering him up. "Stay there, bad boy."

Linda and Rob, waited for some sign indicating Vincent's reaction. All was quiet, after another half hour they took a look and saw he had remained in bed as placed and he had fallen asleep. "He's learned quickly, as they said he might." Rob said proudly.

Linda placed Phyllis in her crib on the far side of the room , covered her up and turned on the baby monitor as they left the room. Half an hour later they heard crying emanating from the nursery. Rushing up and turning on the light they saw little Vincent had climbed out of his crib and crossed the room, where he had pulled Phyllis's arm out through the railings and he was hitting her hand.

Linda reacted swiftly pulling Vincent away from the crib, and putting him back in his crib. "We have to separate them Rob, we can't have them in here together."

Rob agreed, "I'll move Vincent into the spare room tomorrow, tonight Phyllis can sleep with us."

Linda answered " I'm telling you Rob, we have a problem brewing here." She finished with "so much for the perfect child we were promised."

"Don't worry, he'll learn wrong from right" the look on his face was not as encouraging.

Vincent's behavior improved in a backhanded fashion, he interacted less and less with his parents and almost completely ignored Phyllis. He began playing in the backyard and curiously checking on how everything functioned. "He's has an engineering aptitude!" Commented Rob, " He will do well!"

5 Years later

The Flett family functioned as well as most, Phyllis blossomed into a loving, caring daughter.

Vincent still aloof began to interact with his parents, he exhibited traits of high competitiveness and challenged his parents to keep him occupied. He was mastering chess to the point he was equal to Rob, who had been a college champion player. In school, within six months of starting, the teachers advanced him to grade three. Even there, he was without doubt intellectually superior. The only factor holding him back was his inability to work closely with others. He had no concept of team spirit. On the sports field he would singlehandedly maneuver around the opposition team and run up embarrassingly high scores. His coaches admonished him for being too aggressive and he ignored them and became belligerent when they disciplined him by benching him. There was no doubt that scholastically and athletically Vincent was one in a million.

His final evaluation at the clinic had Dr. Sealmann beaming with pride; in his mind his firm had indeed created the 'perfect child'. Vincent's prowess and progress was their showpiece and evidence that cloning could indeed produce superior children and that the world would benefit greatly from their contribution to society.

Cloning activity began increasing at an annualized rate of 30% as more parents wished to have super babies in their families. The trend was set. There was no stopping the development frenzy that public companies were exhibiting in setting up clinics and research facilities to meet the demand for cloning services. At $200,000 a pop, the profit margins were astounding, the risk to the companies low, and the hype amongst the populace continued as designer babies were the 'must have' family addition.

CHAPTER 8

15 Years Later

The Flett family was winding up the family unit. Rob and Linda now approaching their mid sixties were retired from their professions.

Phyllis had completed her nurse's training with honors and was offered a position with a prestigious hospital for sick children. However, she accepted a lesser position with a local hospital because she chose to stay in close contact with her parents.

Vincent had skyrocketed to prominence and obtained an advanced degree in genetic engineering in addition to a Medical Specialist in obstetrics. He joined the firm that had been instrumental in his cloning, Dynamic Cloning Inc. He simplified and streamlined operations to the point where it was now financially possible for most families to consider cloning as the main family planning choice.

The western world was reaching the point where 35% of the general population were cloned individuals, and the percentage of cloned individuals in government, politics and public corporations was approaching 60%. In short robot-like clones controlled every aspect of society. Universities were run by high IQ clones, as were Judges, cloned hospital administrators made life and death choices, the military , the religious groups the United Nations, and the entertainment industry networked to ensure consistent and pointed information was dispensed to the general populace.. Every facet of society was greatly influenced by cloned individuals; practical decision-making was the order of the day. Emotions such as compassion, understanding and kindness were swept aside in favor of results oriented emotionless procedures.

Gradually the population was groomed to accept the concept of self-sacrifice for the good of the country. The 55 plus 1 act was passed, which meant that anyone reaching that age was automatically "removed" from society

The figure of 55 was arrived at by assessing a person's usefulness to society, as a working person, the cost of health care for over 60 year Old's and finally obligations to children who would be grown up by the time parents attained that age. Everyone had to bite the proverbial bullet and have his or her life end one day after their 65th birth date. The reason for the one-day grace was also evident; no one wished to die before his or her final birthday party.

Each day a lovely website list appeared on the internet called "Champions of The Day "showing the names of all good world citizens who complied with the 55 plus 1 law. It was indexed by country, city and street so it was easy to determine just where each Champion originated.

Rob was downing his fifth rum and coke drink, when the seriousness of the moment finally sank in. By tomorrow noon he would be incinerator fire, smoke and ash.. This give a new meaning to the phrase of "High Noon," a hold over from the Gary Cooper 1952 movie title. Cooper with courage and straight shooting extradited himself from his situation. Rob was not accorded such an opportunity nor did he have the necessary skills to save himself. Or did he?

Perhaps Vincent with his influential ways could arrange an exemption for his dad? He placed a call to Dynamics and as usual was asked to leave a message. Rob did, "Hi Son, I am under the gun here with this 55 plus one rule, can you help me out here? Love Dad."

As he stood in his back yard garden party on a beautiful mid summer day gazing out over the blue Pacific ocean, listening to the lively band music, with his wife Linda and daughter Phyllis his mind raced to find a solution to his dilemma. Live or die. It was that simple, yet that complicated.

Rob felt embarrassed and ashamed at the same time. Did not his brother Rodney make the ultimate sacrifice just two years ago, as well as several cousins and friends and his parents some 10 years ago? He had been indoctrinated into the belief of serving the greater good as the "Law" required, yet Rob harbored the desire to circumvent the law to save himself. Selfish? Yes, most would call it that.

It was now eleven p.m. The party guests, knew the routine. One by one they quietly took off their party hats, put down their drinks , stopped joking around, gathered up their belongings and became somber. They dutifully came up to Rob standing at the side gate wishing him a final goodbye as they left. They had done this before, in fact most people attended at least one "final" birthday every month some times two and in a few cases final parties for twins. It was their sworn duty and they obliged, knowing all too well their turn was coming. Few words were spoken, few tears were shed, after all the law was the law. It was necessary to provide space for the children and for grand-children. This was reality in the 21st century. The law had to be obeyed.

The party was over, at midnight . Rob retired to the living room. The phone rang, it was Vincent, "Hi Dad, how are you doing?"

"Getting nervous son, you know this damn 55 plus one law, and it's midnight. Can you do anything for your Dad?"

Vincent paused,"Dad, all I can say is, I love you." The line went dead.

There was a knock on the door. Through the window blinds, Rob saw red and blue lights flashing on police cars parked in the driveway. Linda and Phyllis huddled with Rob comforting him as a second demanding knock sounded.

The time had come; Rob walked dutifully to the door, opened it, stepped out, and surrendered.

The End

Made in the USA
Charleston, SC
26 January 2014